ANDREW LAU AND ALAN MAK'S
Infernal Affairs
– The Trilogy

T0351393

Hong Kong University Press thanks Xu Bing for writing the Press's name in his Square Word Calligraphy for the covers of its books. For further information see p. iv.

THE NEW HONG KONG CINEMA SERIES

The New Hong Kong Cinema came into existence under very special circumstances, during a period of social and political crisis resulting in a change of cultural paradigms. Such critical moments have produced the cinematic achievements of the early Soviet cinema, neorealism, the *nouvelle vague*, and the German cinema of the 1970s and, we can now say, the New Hong Kong Cinema. If this cinema grew increasingly intriguing in the 1980s, after the announcement of Hong Kong's return to China, it is largely because it had to confront a new cultural and political space that was both complex and hard to define, where the problems of colonialism were uncannily overlaid with those of globalism. Such uncanniness could not be caught through straight documentary or conventional history writing: it was left to the cinema to define it.

Has the creative period of the New Hong Kong Cinema now come to an end? However we answer the question, there is a need to evaluate the achievements of Hong Kong cinema. This series distinguishes itself from the other books on the subject by focusing in-depth on individual Hong Kong films, which together make the New Hong Kong Cinema.

Series General Editors
Ackbar Abbas, Wimal Dissanayake, Mette Hjort, Gina Marchetti, Stephen Teo

Series Advisors
Chris Berry, Nick Browne, Ann Hui, Leo Lee, Li Cheuk-to, Patricia Mellencamp, Meaghan Morris, Paul Willemen, Peter Wollen, Wu Hung

Other titles in the series

Fruit Chan's *Durian Durian* by Wendy Gan

John Woo's *A Better Tomorrow* by Karen Fang

King Hu's *A Touch of Zen* by Stephen Teo

Stanley Kwan's *Center Stage* by Mette Hjort

Tsui Hark's *Zu: Warriors From the Magic Mountain* by Andrew Schroeder

Wong Kar-wai's *Ashes of Time* by Wimal Dissanayake

Wong Kar-wai's *Happy Together* by Jeremy Tambling

ANDREW LAU AND ALAN MAK'S
Infernal Affairs
– The Trilogy

Gina Marchetti

香港大學出版社

HONG KONG UNIVERSITY PRESS

Hong Kong University Press
14/F Hing Wai Centre
7 Tin Wan Praya Road
Aberdeen
Hong Kong

© Hong Kong University Press 2007

ISBN 978-962-209-801-5

British Library Cataloguing-in-Publication Data
A catalogue record for this book is available from the British Library.

Secure on-line Ordering
http://www.hkupress.org

Printed and bound by Condor Production Ltd., Hong Kong, China

Hong Kong University Press is honoured that Xu Bing, whose
art explores the complex themes of language across cultures,
has written the Press's name in his Square Word Calligraphy.
This signals our commitment to cross-cultural thinking and the
distinctive nature of our English-language books published in
China.

"At first glance, Square Word Calligraphy appears to be nothing
more unusual than Chinese characters, but in fact it is a new
way of rendering English words in the format of a square so they
resemble Chinese characters. Chinese viewers expect to be able
to read Square Word Calligraphy but cannot. Western viewers,
however are surprised to find they can read it. Delight erupts
when meaning is unexpectedly revealed."

— Britta Erickson, *The Art of Xu Bing*

Contents

Series Preface

The New Hong Kong cinema came into existence under very special circumstances, during a period of social and political crisis resulting in a change of cultural paradigms. Such critical moments have produced the cinematic achievements of the early Soviet cinema, neorealism, the *nouvelle vague*, the German cinema in the 1970s and, we can now say, the recent Hong Kong cinema. If this cinema grew increasingly intriguing in the 1980s, after the announcement of Hong Kong's return to China, it was largely because it had to confront a new cultural and political space that was both complex and hard to define, where the problems of colonialism were overlaid with those of globalism in an uncanny way. Such uncanniness could not be caught through straight documentary or conventional history writing; it was left to the cinema to define it.

It does so by presenting to us an urban space that slips away if we try to grasp it too directly, a space that cinema coaxes into existence by whatever means at its disposal. Thus it is by eschewing a narrow idea of relevance and pursuing disreputable genres like melodrama, kung fu and the fantastic that cinema brings into view something else about the city which could otherwise be missed. One classic example is Stanley Kwan's *Rouge*, which draws on the unrealistic form of the ghost story to evoke something of the uncanniness of Hong Kong's urban space. It takes a ghost to catch a ghost.

In the new Hong Kong cinema, then, it is neither the subject matter nor a particular set of generic conventions that is paramount. In fact, many Hong Kong films begin by following generic conventions but proceed to transform them. Such transformation of genre is also the transformation of a sense of place where all the rules have quietly and deceptively changed. It is this shifting sense of place, often expressed negatively and indirectly — but in the best work always rendered precisely in (necessarily) innovative images — that is decisive for the New Hong Kong Cinema.

Has the creative period of the New Hong Kong Cinema come to an end? However we answer the question, there is a need now to evaluate the achievements of Hong Kong cinema. During the last few years, a number of full-length books have appeared, testifying to the topicality of the subject. These books survey the field with varying degrees of success, but there is yet an almost complete lack of authoritative texts focusing in depth on individual Hong Kong films. This book series on the New Hong Kong Cinema is designed to fill this lack. Each volume will be written by a scholar/ critic who will analyse each chosen film in detail and provide a critical apparatus for further discussion including filmography and bibliography.

Our objective is to produce a set of interactional and provocative readings that would make a self-aware intervention into modern Hong Kong culture. We advocate no one theoretical position; the authors will approach their chosen films from their own distinct points of vantage and interest. The aim of the series is to generate open-ended discussions of the selected films, employing diverse analytical strategies, in order to urge the readers towards self-reflective engagements with the films in particular and the Hong Kong cultural space in general. It is our hope that this series will contribute to the sharpening of Hong Kong culture's conceptions of itself.

In keeping with our conviction that film is not a self-enclosed signification system but an important cultural practice among similar others, we wish to explore how films both reflect and inflect culture. And it is useful to keep in mind that reflection of reality and reality of reflection are equally important in the understanding of cinema.

Ackbar Abbas
Wimal Dissanayake

Acknowledgements

I am particularly grateful to my editor at Hong Kong University Press, Colin Day, who is a man of remarkable vision and energy with a sincere commitment to Hong Kong film. I also would like to thank the New Hong Kong Cinema Series editors, Stephen Teo, Mette Hjort, Wimal Dissanayake, and Ackbar Abbas for their support of this volume. I called on the good will and sharp eyes of several people while writing this book, and I owe a debt of gratitude to Yau Ka-fai, Amy Lee, Staci Ford, Thomas Podvin, and David Vivier for looking at various stages of the manuscript and offering suggestions. Thomas and David's enthusiasm for *Infernal Affairs* and their hard work at *Hong Kong CineMagic* has been an inspiration. I am also very grateful for Steve Fore's perceptive comments on the manuscript. Further thanks go to Charles Leary and the folks at Media Asia for help procuring stills, as well as to Phoebe Chan at Hong Kong University Press for her dedication to this project.

When I first began to work on Hong Kong cinema, Tony Rayns, Ian Jarvie, Ming Tam, Li Cheuk-To, Norman Wang, Roger Garcia,

Evans Chan, Allen Fong, Ho Chi-Kuan, Vivian Huang, Peggy Chiao, Yeh Yueh-Yu, and Yang Ming-Yu were incredibly generous with their knowledge and time. I am always inspired by my colleagues in Asian cinema, including Chris Berry, Jenny Lau, Esther Yau, Joelle Collier, Peter Rist, Jyotika Virdi, Kathe Geist, Linda Ehrlich, George Semsel, Tony Williams, Lalitha Gopalan, Priya Jaikumar, Aaron Park, Adam Knee, Sheldon Lu, Anne Ciecko, Suzie Young, Curtis Tsui, Cindy Wong, Peter Hitchcock, Yau Ching, Patricia Erens, Manju Pendakur, Frances Gateward, David Desser, and Tan See-Kam as well as my colleagues in Asian American film, including Peter X Feng, Phebe Chao, Sumiko Higashi, Marina Heung, Katrien Jacobs, Tad Doyle, John Woo, Jeff Yang, and Darrell Hamamoto.

I am also grateful for the support of so many people here at the University of Hong Kong, including Staci Ford, Priscilla Roberts, Maureen Sabine, Peter Cunich, Jeremy Tambling, Gordon Slethaug, Karen Joe Laidler and Esther Cheung. Richard Stites and Lance Sung made my time in the Fulbright program particularly worthwhile.

I am always inspired by Chuck Kleinhans, Julia Lesage, John Hess, Robert Kolker and Patricia Zimmermann, and I am forever grateful for their friendship. My family is a constant pillar of support, and I could do nothing without Cao Dongqing and Cao Lujia (Luca). In fact, I called upon Dongqing to help with the Chinese film credits and he spent hours on this task. I am forever grateful for his help with this project and for being the love of my life.

Introduction:
The New Wave and the Generic Abyss

A classic story of cops, robbers, and the difficulty of telling them apart, *Infernal Affairs* deals with the tale of two moles — one a triad in the police force and the other an undercover officer in the gangs. As a figure of the imagination, the mole has taken hold on global screens. The character embodies the predicament of hidden and uncertain identities, concealed motives, moral ambiguity, conflicted loyalties, and the inability to take a stand or find roots in an increasingly complex world of new technologies and post-industrial, transnational economies. With the added factors of its change of sovereignty from British to Chinese rule, the Asian financial crisis, and SARS, Hong Kong's obsession with the hidden malevolence behind the quotidian exterior takes on a particular local significance as well, and, in a film industry plagued by triads and the infiltration of Hollywood product, the mole symbolizes the alien within the familiar — the competitor or the parasite within the ranks.

When *Infernal Affairs* appeared in Hong Kong cinemas in 2002, the film industry had been in decline for several years.

Competition from an increasingly aggressive Hollywood distribution system, the infiltration of the triads into the industry in the 1990s, the impact of satellite television, videos, and video piracy, the "brain drain" that had sucked talent from all sectors of the Hong Kong economy including the film industry since the signing of the Joint Declaration in 1984, and the continuing uncertainty of the consequences of the change in sovereignty in 1997 all fed the crisis at the box-office. Emerging at a time when Hong Kong was shaken by SARS, a depressed economy, and waves of political disaffection culminating in the July 1, 2003 demonstrations, the *Infernal Affairs* trilogy speaks to the times. The challenges facing the Hong Kong film industry during this period mirror not only Hong Kong's economic and political problems, but a more general global crisis of labor, national political authority, social structure, cultural authenticity, and personal identity at the turn of the century. In *City on Fire: Hong Kong Cinema*, Lisa Odham Stokes and Michael Hoover note:

> In various ways Hong Kong cinema is revealed to be "crisis cinema," one that finds itself in a historic conjuncture where new patterns of language, time and space, place and identity, and meaning itself, are emerging.[1]

As part of this crisis cinema culture, *Infernal Affairs* holds up a mirror to the industry that created it, the local society that spawned it, as well as the global market that embraced it.

The Internet, video piracy, corporate raiding, and the rise of the remake have been able to "white-wash" Asian popular cinema for a wider Euro-American audience. There is a need to appeal to a "young and dangerous" global youth audience by moving to a new generation of Hong Kong film stars while maintaining the established "brand" of recognizable faces. Not surprisingly, along with other Asian box-office hits like *The Ring* (1998), *My Sassy*

Girl (2001), and *The Eye* (2002), *Infernal Affairs* has been snatched up, not for distribution in the United States, but to be remade by Martin Scorsese into *The Departed* (2006, starring Jack Nicholson, Matt Damon and Leonardo DiCaprio). Fantasies, like capital, commodities, and labor, circulate globally, and *Infernal Affairs*, itself indebted to a slew of Hollywood creations, including *The Godfather Trilogy* (1972–90), *Heat* (1995), *Internal Affairs* (1990), *Miami Vice* (1984–89), *The Sopranos* (1999–2006), and, of course, John Woo's *Face/Off* (1997), provides a case study of how films travel as popular narratives and as commercial products.

Taken as a whole, the *Infernal Affairs* trilogy provides the illusion of an epic sweep (from 1991–2003) that covers the issues of government legitimacy, global capitalist expansion, individual alienation, and the implosion of a system that blurs "legitimate" political authority with an underground "illegitimate" economic reality. As part of the New Hong Kong Cinema Series, this short book attempts to highlight the significance of *Infernal Affairs* within the context of contemporary Hong Kong cinema as well as within global film culture by examining all three films in the trilogy. Exploring the way *Infernal Affairs* has crossed borders as a story, a commercial product, and as a work of art, this study demonstrates the ways in which Hong Kong cinema continues to be inextricably intertwined with global film culture and the transnational movie market.

Infernal Affairs touches on themes hotly debated within contemporary critical theory, including globalization, transnational migrations and diaspora, the politics of time and space, nostalgia, memory and the archive, consumerism and post-industrial capitalism, identity and subjectivity, new technologies of communication, and the defining qualities of postmodernity. The trilogy conjures up a narrative time and space intersected by rings, like the circles of hell, of aesthetic, cultural, historical, political, and economic associations. After peeling away these layers, including the trilogy's relationship to popular genres, spatial/ temporal structure, its use of allegory, its reliance on performance, its association with the Hong Kong New Wave, and its commercial ties to Greater Chinese cinema, this analysis of *Infernal Affairs* concludes with a look at the trilogy's self-reflexive allusions to the mass media and the current state of Hong Kong film culture within a global context.

Infernal Affairs and the New Wave

Current Hong Kong cinema runs the gamut from commercial genre films through the Hong Kong New Wave and the "Second Wave" of newer directors to the work of independent filmmakers who often collaborate with or are influenced by the Sixth Generation from the People's Republic of China (PRC). *Infernal Affairs*, with its star-studded cast and high production values, adheres more to the commercial end of that spectrum. However, in Hong Kong film culture, the boundaries between the commercial, the art house, and the experimental blur, and filmmakers may move from film school experimentation to public-financed television to commercial features to art house productions or independent co-productions throughout the course of their careers. For example, John Woo went from making experimental shorts as part of Hong Kong's cine-club movement to working for Chang Cheh at Shaw Brothers, to being part of Hong Kong's New Wave through his association with Tsui Hark, to crossing the Pacific to make commercial Hollywood features.[2]

Although *Infernal Affairs'* "new cinema" credentials may be a bit shaky, they are worth examining to provide an entry into the way the film circulates globally as popular entertainment with art film overtones. As Charles Leary has noted:

The hyperbolic tale of police corruption — i.e. corruption among those investigating corruption (the Internal Affairs office) — might also invite a constellation between this new image of Hong Kong "high concept" cinema in *Infernal Affairs* and a flashback to the Hong Kong new wave of the 1980s, some of whose noted auteurs honed their skills by making docudramas for a television series sponsored by Hong Kong's Independent Commission Against Corruption.[3]

In fact, several associations link the cast and crew of *Infernal Affairs* with the Hong Kong New Wave. Andrew Lau Wai-keung, *Infernal Affairs'* co-director and cinematographer, has moved between art films and commercial features throughout his career. Both his art house projects and his commercial forays, in fact, have dealt with criminals and police. He worked with Wong Kar-wai as his cinematographer on two stories of cops and crooks, *As Tears Go By* (1988) and *Chungking Express* (1994), as well as working behind the camera for Ringo Lam on a story of an undercover mole, *City on Fire* (1987).

Lau directed *To Live and Die in Tsimshatsui* (1994)[4] with the prolific and unabashedly commercial Wong Jing.[5] *To Live and Die in Tsimshatsui*, like *Infernal Affairs*, deals with an undercover cop with an identity crisis. Continuing to work within the triad genre, Lau moved on to youth gangs in the *Young and Dangerous* series (beginning in 1996). With this background, Lau has had plenty of experience blending triad pulp fiction with New Wave stylistic and thematic concerns around the mole — moving effortlessly between the influence of Wong Jing and Wong Kar-wai.

For *Infernal Affairs*, for example, Lau drew on Wong Kar-wai regular, Christopher Doyle, to provide some assistance with the color timing in the processing lab, so that the film exhibits a Hong Kong New Wave texture. The look of the film, in fact, resonates with a visual style that has helped to define the Hong Kong New Wave for a global audience. Combining the grittiness of location shooting with the élan of contrasting colors and textures, the cinematography ranges from electronically manipulated video images to soft black and white as well as drained and saturated colors. Cool exterior blues and neon toned greens, cold metallic shades for institutional interiors, and warm browns and earth tones for intimate interiors round out the palette.

As in other Hong Kong New Wave films, *Infernal Affairs* does not shy away from placing cinematographic virtuosity in the foreground — including dramatic contrasts of field size (moving between extreme close-ups of facial details to extreme long shots of the Hong Kong cityscape), height (going from the tops of skyscrapers to cluttered depths of the city's markets), and movement (from dynamic pans to nearly imperceptible re-framings of virtually static tableaux). Camera movement and editing work together to establish a rhythm that fluctuates violently throughout the film — from periods of quiet contemplation to moments of frenetic violence. This visual pace follows the twists and turns of the narrative that moves without a fixed spatial or temporal anchor. In fact, *Infernal Affairs'* co-director/co-writer Alan Mak Siu-fai experimented with elliptical narratives reminiscent of many Hong Kong New Wave films in *Rave Fever* (1999), and the same vertiginous disregard for classical continuity characterizes the trilogy.

In front of the camera, the acting talents also have strong New Wave credentials. Andy Lau worked with Wong Kar-wai as a young thug in *As Tears Go By* and as a cop in *Days of Being Wild* (1991), and Tony Leung has been a staple in Wong Kar-wai's films from *Ashes of Time* and *Chungking Express* (both 1994) through *2046* (2004). Leung and Lau have worked with Hong Kong New Wave, Taiwan New Cinema, and Fifth Generation Chinese directors such as Ann Hui, Stanley Kwan, Hou Hsiao-Hsien, and Zhang Yimou. Andy Lau produced independent director Fruit Chan's *Made in Hong Kong* (1997) and *The Longest Summer* (1998) and co-produced *Infernal Affairs*. Supporting actors Eric Tsang and Anthony Wong have credits working with edgy directors including Wayne Wang, Allen Fong, Peter Chan, and Sylvia Chang. In 2003, both Tsang and Wong were featured in the independent *Fu Bo*. Other supporting actors have also worked for independent filmmakers — e.g., Hu Jun starred in Zhang Yuan's *East Palace, West Palace* (1996).[6]

Survival in transnational Chinese cinema has depended on cultivating and maintaining "flexible"[7] identities (like the moles in *Infernal Affairs'* fiction). Chinese filmmakers (from the PRC, Hong Kong, Taiwan, and elsewhere) move between art and commerce, between European film festivals and American art houses, with dreams of Hollywood remakes or multiplex breakthroughs. For example, Taiwan director Ang Lee, via his proxy Jen (Zhang Ziyi), takes a leap of faith into an abyss that may bring the rewards of enlightenment or the obscurity of oblivion in *Crouching Tiger Hidden Dragon* (2000). In *Hero* (2002), mainland Chinese director Zhang Yimou also takes a chance through his proxy Nameless (Jet Li) that the world is ready for the return of the wandering hero — Nameless/Jet Li who travels from the PRC to Hong Kong to Hollywood and back again to China. *Hero* also imaginatively repatriates Hong Kong's Tony Leung (as Broken Sword) and Maggie Cheung (as Flying Snow) as well as Chinese-American Donnie Yen (as Sky) who sacrifice themselves to maintain the Chinese nation-state. The diasporic Chinese from the far edges of the world symbolically capitulate to the central authority of the Emperor Qin (Chen Daoming)/Beijing/the PRC/Chinese cinema.[8]

While Lee and Zhang put their resources into the re-imagined "community" of dynastic China, Lau and Mak rework the contemporary crime genre by mingling the gangster/triad film with the police story. However, just as Lee draws on Hong Kong, PRC and American talent to make his Taiwanese version of a Hong Kong action film set in mainland China, and Zhang pulls in actors from the far reaches of Greater China for his version of the Hong Kong martial arts film made in the PRC, Lau and Mak create a Hong Kong film in tune with transnational flows. For *Infernal Affairs III*, for example, the directors snatched up Chen Daoming, who plays the Qin Emperor in Zhang's *Hero*, to embody Mainland authority as the police mole Shen (a.k.a. "Shadow" — a reference to the Chinese word for "cinema" — *dian ying*/"electric shadows"), while Zhang Yimou cast Andy Lau as a duplicitous mole in his period martial arts film *House of Flying Daggers* (2004). Directors from Taiwan, Hong Kong, and the PRC, working on the edges of the international art film/commercial film marketplace, draw on the same pool of Greater Chinese onscreen talent, generic conventions, and thematic concerns.

If both *Crouching Tiger Hidden Dragon* and *Hero* play with the idea of the abyss (oblivion of the void/destructive force of empire) and the loss of self (sacrifice of the body for spiritual enlightenment or of individual independence for national unity), *Infernal Affairs* makes those themes explicit from the outset. The film is the "dao" (way) of "wu jian" (no place/nowhere) — the impossible path of Buddhist "continuous hell." Just as Lee and Zhang take a leap of faith by bringing their martial arts characters to the abyss, Lau and Mak follow suit by bringing their characters into the inferno, hoping for a commercial rebirth from the generic ashes.

2

Forgotten Times:
Music, Memory, Time, and Space

After going their separate ways from the police academy, Chan (Tony Leung) and Lau (Andy Lau) meet in a stereo store. Neither recognizes the other (Still 2.1). Chan, who exploits the store for protection money and uses it as a drug drop, plays the role of proprietor, when the owner steps out. Lau, off-duty, dressed neatly in a button-down shirt, takes on the persona of consumer/connoisseur, credit card at the ready, in the store to purchase a stereo for the apartment he must furnish for his bride. For a moment, they can "forget" to be cops and robbers. The cop who pretends to be a gangster, dressed in a leather jacket, can be the "honest" proprietor. In fact, Chan gives Lau a deal on the equipment

Still 2.1 *Infernal Affairs:* Lau and Chan in stereo store

and a tip to buy speakers at another store where he can get a better price. When the real owner returns, he is furious, of course, since he needs to mark up the price to pay the triads protection money.

Likewise, the gangster who pretends to be the cop can be the savvy consumer. Lau even suggests that Chan add a particular piece of equipment to the set-up to enhance his appreciation of the "oldies" he enjoys. Given that Andy Lau serves as a government spokesperson for the honest and courteous treatment of consumers in Hong Kong, this scene plays with another element of identity by allowing Andy Lau and Tony Leung to model the ideal business transaction. Ironically, "honest" commerce is conducted by actors playing characters playing moles. It takes a fake to appreciate the genuine article.

This scene also introduces the relationship between technology, economics, and the films' plot. The *Infernal Affairs* trilogy pictures new technologies — from computers and cell phones to the latest in home entertainment. Stereo equipment is spread out before Chan and Lau, and the two take their seats side by side to listen and appreciate the aural subtleties the sound technology can offer to them — "Human voices are drifting toward you" (Still 2.2). They

Still 2.2   *Infernal Affairs:* Lau and Chan in stereo store

survey the riches of Hong Kong electronics — American, Japanese, and European technology brought together with labor from China into the Hong Kong marketplace. Hong Kong acts as an entrepôt — a point of repackaging and transshipment. The stereo store serves as a micro version, a case study, of the postwar Hong Kong economy.[1]

In addition to being a key commodity in Hong Kong's mercantile profile, the stereo represents "cultural capital"[2] that the Hong Kong middle-classes can both appreciate and afford. Chan and Lau buy into it as a sign of their affluence and taste. Lau pays with a credit card, and Chan adroitly processes the transaction. Lau has made it in Hong Kong — he not only can afford a stereo, he has proven himself a fit candidate for credit. Even Chan, who operates presumably as both a police officer and a gangster within a cash economy — off the books on the police payroll as well as in the triad's accounts — understands credit and the status it confers. The card signifies an identity beyond Chan's reach, and a need that cash cannot seem to satisfy. Later in *Infernal Affairs I,*[3] Chan is dwarfed by images of happy consumers wielding credit cards while he struggles simply to stay alive (Still 2.3).

Still 2.3 *Infernal Affairs:* Chan and advertising posters

Adding the hidden drugs in one component of the stereo floor display, the scene becomes a picture of both the legitimate and "unofficial," hidden economy of Hong Kong — capitalism in the light of day and the dark of night (Still 2.4). Both Chan and Lau, as cops and criminals, aspire to the same bourgeois dream — a legitimate profession or business, a credit card in hand, a wife and child in the fully furnished, electronically up-to-date flat. The stereo concretizes that dream they both understand and try desperately to attain. Taken together, they create a portrait of the model Hong Kong subject — the bureaucrat and the entrepreneur.

Still 2.4 *Infernal Affairs III:*
drugs in stereo

In addition to providing a picture of commerce, this scene also paints a portrait of Hong Kong's political economy. The criminal pretending to be a cop and the cop pretending to be a criminal merge into one system — rooted in "legitimate" colonial control and the legacy of illegal triad activities. With triad roots in secret political agitation against dynastic rule and police roots in British colonialism and the forced opening of Chinese markets to drugs, both arise from the same history of oppression, corruption, and decadence. After 1997 and Hong Kong's intermediate status as an SAR under PRC sovereignty, their identities become even less certain, and their missions less clear. They both long to "forget" their identities — as representatives of the state or representatives of forces opposed to the state or both — and luxuriate in their "true" vocations as small businessmen and consumers — buyers and sellers in the Hong Kong marketplace.

Lau and Chan share a common vision of middleclass-ness. They both attempt to construct an identity solidly within the professional/small business sphere as midlevel bureaucrats and small-scale shop owners. The fact that these identities are false does not belie the truth that both men hold these fantasies/

delusions/masks very dear. Shopping has a quasi-religious ritualized quality, and organizing commodities carefully for display (e.g., in the shop or in Lau's honeymoon apartment) enhances their fetishistic qualities. They carefully craft their identities through commodities — from stereo equipment and popular music to furniture, clothing, cell phones, and watches.

Shopping reverberates transnationally across media. For example, David Chase articulates his vision for the last year of his gangster cable television series *The Sopranos* within the overarching theme of consumerism:

> I started thinking about what are these people really about, what are they really after ... It's going to be about money and about materialism, buying stuff, consumerism ... . That's all they care about. All that stuff helps them not to think about larger issues. I notice that myself. When I go shopping, I feel better. It's like a high.[4]

The characters in *The Sopranos* as well as the protagonists in *Infernal Affairs* share, with their audiences in Hong Kong and abroad, a common idealized identity and create a global community based on a common culture of consumerism. They are part of the same global niche market for specialized goods — a market within which DVDs of *Infernal Affairs* circulate among Hong Kong film fans globally through Internet commerce. Lisa Odham Stokes and Michael Hoover characterize this class as follows:

> ... a professional-managerial stratum that helps to make capital more mobile can be observed wearing, drinking, and driving the same international brands as they watch the same cosmopolitan movies and listen to the same popular music.[5]

Ending the trilogy with a return to the scene in the stereo store reinforces this bond with the audience — a bourgeois dream of consumption in which the identities of Lau/Andy Lau and Chan/ Tony Leung become part of a global marketplace of profitable dreams.

Lau and Chan bond while listening to a recording of Tsai Chin singing "Forgotten Times."[6] Directors Lau and Mak say the song is a bit of serendipity. The technician used the recording to check the sound equipment on the set, and the directors decided to use it.[7] Chance, then, provides structure for the entire trilogy. The song conjures up the 1980s, the time before the beginning of the story in 1991, and the haunting melody and lyrics invite nostalgic reverie. It sets up key aural motifs through its later association with both Marys (the loves of Lau's life), Chan's "tapping" (the Morse code used to communicate with his superior/an action mentioned in the song's lyrics), and references to "forgotten" times (the film's repeated use of flashbacks to the police academy and the triad initiation ceremony — "forgotten"/repressed memories that haunt both protagonists).[8] The lyrics ask the key question "who?" — echoing the trilogy's preoccupation with questions of identity. The song refers to memory and time — themes central to the unfolding of the narrative. In "Maps, Movies, Musics and Memory," Iain Chambers touches on the power music can have in film to conjure up questions of time, space, and memory:

> Music permits us to travel: forward in fantasy, backward in time, sideways in speculation. Above all, music draws us into the passages of memory ... The time of memory is a reversible time that permits the return, revisiting and revision of other times. The coeval presence of this reversible time and the irreversible nature of our bodies opens up a rent in our experience, in our lives. Linear, irrevocable time is interrupted by the interval and intrusion of transversal times: the genealogy of the symptom, of recall, of the recording and reordering of the past, and the perpetual desire to return to the record.[9]

"Forgotten Times" provides a musical map throughout the trilogy that keeps these issues of movement, transformation, memory, time, identity, performance, and loss in the foreground.

With its association with narrative breaks and alienated characters, "Forgotten Times" insists that *Infernal Affairs'* New Wave connections not be ignored. Extratextual links come into play. The chanteuse Tsai Chin was married to Taiwan New Cinema director Edward Yang,[10] starred in his film *Taipei Story* (1985) with two other Taiwan New Cinema directors, Hou Hsiao-Hsien and Wu Nien-Jen, and also starred in Hong Kong Second Wave director Stanley Kwan's *Love unto Waste* (1986). In fact, she worked with Tony Leung in the Kwan film. (Christopher Doyle provides another connection to Taiwan's Edward Yang. Doyle started his career working on Yang's *That Day, On the Beach*, 1983.)

Listening to Tsai Chin, Andy Lau and Tony Leung sit as actors appreciating a fellow performer. Chan and Lau slide into the background, and the fact that the film takes performance as a key theme comes to the fore. However, if Fredric Jameson characterized another film by Edward Yang, *The Terrorizer* (1986),[11] as existing somewhere between the "modern" and the "postmodern," *Infernal Affairs* fits comfortably within the postmodern. New Wave modernism becomes a disembodied voice, a haunting melody from the past, an element of diegetic sound that begins and ends the tale but remains trapped in the machine, an off-screen commentary on the action rather than a player in the drama.

Lau and Chan side by side in the stereo shop, like the master and guest side-by-side in Hong Kong costume films set in dynastic China, parallel the scene in which Chan and Lau appear to sit side by side in Dr. Lee's office in *Infernal Affairs III* (Still 2.5). Chan and Lau answer her questions identically, merging into a single character for Lee or portraying the disturbed psyche of Lau, giving voice to repressed thoughts. In fact, repression exists at several levels beyond the most superficial one of including a psychiatrist,

Dr. Lee, as a character in the film, who analyzes the protagonists. Chan and Lau need to repress their true identities to survive in a corrupt world, the plot needs to repress the colonial past to carry on with the morality tale of the present, the film needs to repress the New Wave in order to find commercial success in the international film marketplace, and Hong Kong needs to repress Taiwan to get on with forging its new identity as part of the PRC, not the ROC/Taiwan.

Still 2.5 *Infernal Affairs III:* two on a couch

As a song in Mandarin from Taiwan, "Forgotten Times" alludes to both the past and the future. The need to keep Taiwan under wraps points to a political history. It refers to Taiwan's move from martial law, through the end of Kuomingtang (KMT) rule, to a present moment of potentially dangerous calls for an identity independent of the PRC. Associations with Taiwan conjure up a move from one-party rule to a more open political playing field, echoing Hong Kong's own call for greater political autonomy and democratic voice. However, the use of Mandarin also points to a broader Chinese identity, a move from the regional dialect of Cantonese to "guo yu" — the "national language" or "putong hua" — the "common speech" — of a China beyond Hong Kong and a future as part of the PRC.

Cantopop does not define their predicament — although Andy Lau does sing the title song in Cantonese over the credits. Rather, the Taiwan popular ballad, most often identified with the late Teresa Teng, cements Lau and Chan's bond. (In fact, this connection to ROC popular culture is solidified by the cameo appearance of

Taiwanese pop singer Eva Hsiao as May, Chan's ex-girlfriend and the mother of his young daughter.) Lau and Chan consume a Greater Chinese cultural commodity in Mandarin with a Taiwanese accent. The hardware and the software of their personal and economic interaction take them away from a solid center — from both Beijing and Hong Kong defined identities — and put them within a more vertiginous global orbit.

Of course the use of Taiwan's pop culture in this way is nothing new in Hong Kong cinema. Teresa Teng's "Tian Mi Mi" serves a similar function in Peter Chan's *Comrades: Almost a Love Story* (1996) and provides the film with its Chinese title. In fact, the trilogy has several points of contact with Taiwan's film culture. Eric Tsang (Sam in *Infernal Affairs*), for example, plays a Taiwanese gangster in *Comrades*.[12] In Hou's epic film, *City of Sadness* (1989), Tony Leung plays a mute witness to the February 28, 1947, massacre of people who resisted KMT rule over Taiwan.[13] In Wong Kar-wai's *Happy Together* (1997), the character Tony Leung plays, Lai Yiu-fai, ends up in Taipei at the end of the film. Anthony Wong (Superintendent Wong in *Infernal Affairs*) appears regularly in films set in Taiwan directed by Sylvia Chang like *Princess D* (2002) and *20:30:40* (2004). Given the associations between triads and the KMT, gangsters from Taiwan and Hong Kong triad connections to Taiwan are ubiquitous within the genre (e.g., *A Better Tomorrow*, 1986). Andy Lau plays a policeman after triads trying to infiltrate Taiwan politics in Michael and Johnny Mak's *Island of Greed/Black Gold* (1997). Andrew Lau has also brought in the Taiwan triad connections in his *Young and Dangerous* series, and Taiwan's triads figure prominently in *Too Many Ways to Be Number One* (1997), featuring Francis Ng from *Infernal Affairs II*.

In *Infernal Affairs III*, a subplot involves Superintendent Yeung (Leon Lai — a costar in *Comrades: Almost a Love Story*) and a pair of older Taiwanese arms dealers who are repatriated to the PRC for prosecution. The fact that Hong Kong's SAR status revolving around "one country, two systems" had originally been crafted for Taiwan's reunification with the Mainland plays at the edges of the trilogy. *Infernal Affairs*, crafted by two directors, offers one narrative with two protagonists. Chan and Lau are two moles at opposite ends of a geopolitical situation involving state control and economic expediency, and Taiwan's presence in the films underscores this fact.

In "Obtuse Music and Nebulous Males: The Haunting Presence of Taiwan in Hong Kong Films of the 1990s," Shen Shiao-Ying notes "as Hong Kong finds itself at peace with great cultural China, the Taiwan factor becomes redundant and dismissible, but not eradicable."[14] Given that "Forgotten Times" allows Lau and Chan a respite from their hide-and-seek game of deception and that the directors' claim that the choice of this particular song was serendipitous, it may make sense to dismiss the fact this song comes from Taiwan as inconsequential. However, in this essay, Shen makes another point concerning the link between music from Taiwan/Taiwanese characters and a broader crisis of masculinity in several Hong Kong films from the 1990s that may be more difficult to reject.[15]

Chan and Lau listen to a female voice from Taiwan singing in Mandarin — a voice linked to the problem of the Chinese "nation," but also to the question of gender identity. The two men luxuriate in the sound of the woman's voice. In *Infernal Affairs*, women remain at the margins of the narrative — critical to the machinations of the plot, but only as supporting characters. Dr. Lee, the psychiatrist and Chan's love interest, figures the feminine as the repressed — the woman as analyst, object of desire, and key to the "forgotten times" that plague both Chan and Lau.

In addition to the opening and closing scenes in the stereo store, "Forgotten Times" plays at other key moments. In *Infernal Affairs I*, Lau's bride, Mary (Sammi Cheng), learns that the police officer in her life is not quite what he seems when she plays a tape of "Forgotten Times" that includes a conversation with Lau and triad boss Sam. In *Infernal Affairs II*, Sam's wife Mary (Carina Lau) introduces the young Lau (Edison Chen) to the song after he has successfully completed his first gangland assassination. At the end of that film, the song plays when the young Lau meets the new Mary (Chiu Cheng-yue) and falls in love as soon as he hears her name. In *Infernal Affairs III*, the song is found among Lau's effects during an investigation of his office. At the same time, the telephone rings. Mary (Sammi Cheng) has agreed to meet Lau before their divorce proceeds, but he cannot make the meeting, because of his suicide attempt.

"Forgotten Times" connects Lau to both the Marys in his life, and, as revealed in *Infernal Affairs II*, initiates him into the underworld as a murderer. At the end of *Infernal Affairs II*, it acts as a bridge between the two Marys as it comes up when Lau becomes smitten with the new Mary, who, drunk from too much celebrating during the 1997 Handover, ends up in front of Officer Lau unable to spell her name. The song, with the murdered Sam's haunting threat, forces the realization Lau needs/wants to turn his life around and become a genuine cop in *Infernal Affairs I*. Although he may never have realized it, Sam, from the grave, avenges his wife Mary who was killed by Lau because she spurned his advances. "Forgotten Times" merges the two murders, and Lau must deal with the intrusion of the voice of the deceased Sam in order to possess the second Mary in his life and become a "genuine" cop.

Even after the carnage that leaves Lau paralyzed in a sanatorium in *Infernal Affairs III*, "Forgotten Times" emerges from Lau's safe to stop the investigation into his criminal activities within the police force cold (Still 2.6). The song continues to haunt the operations of the police by posing the question of "who?" dares to disturb the "forgotten times" — the times of corruption within their ranks — that should remain repressed. To add another dimension to this, Carina Lau, who plays Sam and Lau's Mary, is Tony Leung's actual, off-screen girlfriend. Associated with the fictitious Lau's on-screen obsession, Mary/Carina, through her connection with "Forgotten Times," conjures up Tony Leung's real romance. On-screen fiction and off-screen life again blur as the two men bond around the figure of the same woman while listening to the same song.

Still 2.6 *Infernal Affairs III:* "Forgotten Times" stops everyone

In the twilight world of the stereo store, listening to Tsai Chin's haunting voice,[16] the mise-en-scène conjures up the uncanny darkness of the tomb as well as the womb. As in the ancient Greek tale of Orpheus and Eurydice in the underworld, music takes on infernal associations. Trapped as Chan and Lau are in "continuous hell," each remains plagued by his own constructed persona; the women fail to represent salvation (as they may have in earlier iterations of the genre). Chan's and Lau's identities have become too fractured to piece together again, and they remain in the perpetual "hell" of an identity crisis over-determined by their questionable ties to the state (Hong Kong police), the economy (transnational drug running), the nation (Hong Kong–PRC–Taiwan/ROC), and their gender. Their inability to take on the role of patriarch points to a crisis in Confucian masculinity. Each leaves a lover to parent his child without him. They also fail to live up to either the brotherhood of the police force or the underworld *jiang hu,* since both betray the people they have become closest to as moles.[17] Chan and Lau fail as men, as Chinese, and as Chinese men. The deceased Chan and the paralyzed Lau represent utter incapacitation, impotence, and the futility of holding on to identities rooted in corrupt and nearly defunct systems — both "legitimate" and "illegal." Chan's broken arm in a cast in the stereo store prefigures the "broken" identities and fractured masculinities of both principals in the trilogy.[18]

Returning to the stereo store at the end of the trilogy, however, allows *Infernal Affairs* to transcend this picture of a "castrated" Hong Kong society "saved" by more efficient mainland police, independent career women, and single mothers. The trilogy ends with "Forgotten Times" and the presentation of global Chinese culture, embodied by the disembodied voice of Tsai Chin, and the physical presence of two of Hong Kong's most bankable transnational stars — Andy Lau and Tony Leung. Like the stereo equipment spread before them, this image puts on display the art and the commerce of Hong Kong cinema for the enjoyment of the local as well as the global viewer.

However, the stereo equipment — bulky and seemingly out of date in the cinematic world of *Infernal Affairs* that operates primarily with cell phones, lap top computers, and miniaturized surveillance cameras — also represents nostalgia for a past technology. In *Infernal Affairs II*, Mary (Carina Lau), who deals in black market stereo equipment, talks about how expensive her old American stereo is and rhapsodizes, "They say this American antique has sweet high, crisp middle and strong bass." She concludes, "Bullshit," and she claims to enjoy the stereo for the status it confers as a rare commodity rather than for the aesthetic pleasure it gives her as a music lover. However, Lau seems smitten with both Tsai Chin's "Forgotten Times" and Mary, not as symbols of status within the triad world, but as aesthetic/romantic/libidinal objects of desire. Mary makes a present of the compact disc to Lau with a promise to get him a decent stereo in the future. The parallel to the cinema cannot be ignored. Playing *Infernal Affairs* on a VCD or DVD may be nice, but it does not beat the old technology of celluloid before the digital revolution. Lau, Chan, Mary, and the film viewer all savor the old technology, while enjoying a plot that revolves around the new world of cell phones, lap top computers, and special effects that blend the old and new.

Nostalgia

Infernal Affairs fits within Fredric Jameson's definition of the "nostalgia film."[19] For Jameson, the "nostalgia film" need not be set in the historical past; rather, its defining characteristic resides in its ability to replicate past styles associated with cultural objects from another era. Although referring to George Lucas's *Star Wars* (1977), Jameson's remarks could easily be applied to the *Infernal Affairs* trilogy as well:

> ... far from being a pointless satire of such now dead forms, satisfies a deep (might I say repressed?) longing to experience them again: it is a complex object in which on some first level children and adolescents can take the adventure straight, while the adult public is able to gratify a deeper and more properly nostalgic desire to return to that older period and live its strange old aesthetic artifacts through once again ... by reinventing the feel and shape of characteristic art objects of an older period ... , it seeks to reawaken a sense of the past associated with those objects.[20]

The reference to the "oldies" of the 1980s goes beyond the political reference to 1984 as a turning point in Hong Kong's identity as a place. The image of Lau and Chan, two stars Andy Lau and Tony Leung, seated together enjoying Greater Chinese popular culture together by listening to a Tsai Chin classic from the 1980s also conjures up images from Hong Kong's cinematic past — specifically, of John Woo's homoerotic buddy films in which cops and crooks bond like Ah Jong/Jeff (Chow Yun-fat) and Inspector Lee (Dannie Lee) in *The Killer* (1989).[21]

References to Woo's oeuvre abound — from several stand-offs with guns pointed point blank throughout the trilogy to one scene in Thailand in *Infernal Affairs II* in which the comic Keung (Chapman To) ineffectually blazes away with a pistol in each hand. Alan Mak has mentioned that he had *Face/Off* (1997)[22] in mind when he scripted *Infernal Affairs* (with Felix Chong).[23] Although the plot echoes *Face/Off*'s obsession with malleable identities that cross moral boundaries of good and evil, the style of the film harkens back to Woo's *A Better Tomorrow* (1986) and also takes up that film's interest in the taint of triad family connections and the way in which filial duty complicates dedication to the state's notion of "law and order."[24] Also made during a downturn in the fortunes of the Hong Kong film industry, *A Better Tomorrow* did deliver on its promise and became the top grossing film of all time in Hong Kong, a position it held for several years after its initial release. It defined a look — duster, sunglasses, and two guns blazing — that helped to delineate the Hong Kong gangster/police hybrid for global audiences. With Ringo Lam's *City on Fire* (1987) and other films about undercover cops and triad moles, *Infernal Affairs* follows in this tradition, building on that hybrid genre, and also delivering a significant profit for its producers.

As "Forgotten Times" makes evident at the end of the trilogy, *Infernal Affairs* promises a "forgotten" filmic pleasure — a revival of Greater Chinese cinematic artistry within mass-mediated popular culture. *Infernal Affairs* obliquely, but insistently, refers to its status as an art object as well as a commercial commodity. As Fredric Jameson notes:

> But this means that contemporary or postmodernist art is going to be about art itself in a new kind of way; even more, it means that one of its essential messages will involve the necessary failure of art and the aesthetic, the failure of the new, the imprisonment in the past.[25]

Without a doubt, *Infernal Affairs* represents a "failure of the new" and "imprisonment in the past." Its plot about two failed protagonists, who do not survive in the contemporary world and appear first and last on screen listening to a song about "forgotten times," makes this abundantly clear on a very basic level. Unlike Chinese-language New Wave films with clearer modernist leanings, *Infernal Affairs* does not cite other works in order to construct a new cinematic vision. Emerging during a slump in the industry, it revives an older style associated with John Woo in the 1980s — itself fashioned out of a pastiche of Hollywood gangsters, spaghetti Western standoffs, Chinese martial arts homoeroticism, Confucianism and Christian notions of chivalry.[26] When one of the gangsters in the Ngai family takes out a harmonica and begins to play during the burial of a rival gangster, for example, *Infernal Affairs II* cites the use of the harmonica in Sergio Leone's *Once Upon a Time in the West* (1969) via John Woo's elegiac moments of triad sentimentality. However, it is precisely that "failure of art and the aesthetic" that has made *Infernal Affairs* a bankable commodity. Remembering and repressing its New Wave connections, "Forgotten Times" highlights that dynamic as it circulates through the film's narrative and keeps in the foreground the fact that *Infernal Affairs* takes up art as a commodity and as a technology as its subject matter.

Screening Time: Time as Commodity/Fetish

At a basic level, commercial cinema turns time into a commodity. The value of the time captured on film, the cost of the labor put into the film's production, translates into the price of the ticket to spend roughly two hours watching the film in the cinema. While, from a Marxist perspective, film as a commodity fetish hides labor, from a Freudian perspective, it employs the fetish to disavow castration. *Infernal Affairs* makes use of both notions of the fetish.[27]

In *Infernal Affairs I*, a commentary on the decline in Hong Kong film's profitability forms part of a scene in which Lau and Chan nearly run into each other at a movie theatre. Chan has trailed Sam to a multiplex, where Sam and Lau meet in the dark. A film that looks like it is set in Mongolia or Tibet (perhaps a minority film from the People's Republic) plays to a near empty house. Sam comments that the women in the film look "ugly," and no one seems to have much interest in what is on screen. The posters for Hollywood films, like *Men in Black II* (2002), in the hallway of the theater, further comment on the sorry state of affairs for Chinese-language films in the Hong Kong marketplace (Still 2.7). For Sam and Lau, a movie house seems a safe bet for a rendezvous, since it is likely to be empty. *Infernal Affairs* attempts to transform that image of cinema time (as boring) and cinema space (as empty) by making a film that turns a profit. Sam's boredom and repulsion at the film within the film turn into the intense editing and quick tempo of Chan's pursuit of Lau — brought to a close by the bad "timing" of Chan's ringing cell phone. Again, as it did with "Forgotten Times," *Infernal Affairs* announces its distance from languid pace of Chinese art cinema by moving away from the films associated with the PRC's Fifth Generation filmmakers like Tian Zhuangzhuang.

Still 2.7 *Infernal Affairs: Men in Black II* poster

If the stereo that plays "Forgotten Times" marks the border between sound as an art form and as a commodity, watches serve a similar function in the *Infernal Affairs* trilogy by marking the boundary between time as a commodity and as a symbol. In *Infernal*

Affairs I, Superintendent Wong gives Chan a watch. At first, Chan thinks it may be some sort of surveillance device, but Wong has simply remembered Chan's birthday with a gift. Throughout the Greater Chinese world (as elsewhere), the watch serves as a typical gift to solidify relationships — boss to employee, parent to graduating student, husband to wife. While the clock (which sounds like the "end" — synonymous with "death" in Chinese) can never be given as a gift without cursing the recipient, the watch (a different word in Chinese) does not connote any ill will. Given that their conversation has revolved around the amount of time Chan has spent undercover (over ten years), the gift concretizes Chan's time spent working as a mole for the triads. Chan has served his time — quite literally in jail as well as figuratively undercover. Since the pre-credit sequence established the fact that Chan does not enjoy working as a mole, this watch crystallizes his alienated labor — the time he has worked without sufficient reward. Disgruntled, Chan remarks, "I never wear watches" (Still 2.8).

Still 2.8   *Infernal Affairs:* watch

In *Infernal Affairs II*, on his way to his first assassination, Lau stops to admire an expensive watch in a shop window. Time exists as a consumer commodity and status symbol. In fact, several of the gangsters in the film flaunt expensive watches to indicate their success. After the killing, Lau meets Mary at her office and admires the gold watch she wears. However, when Lau enquires whether the watch is a gift from Sam, she tells him to mind his own business. Time and timepieces also mark the boundaries of an exclusive relationship. The coveted watch and the coveted woman merge, and Lau wants to control and possess both.

At his desk in the police station, Lau takes off his watch and puts it in front of him on his desk. Lau may be a fake cop, but, as a gangster, he can have a "real" Rolex. He notes his time working for the police as well as the triads as he multi-tasks doing paperwork for the government and spying for Sam. Official time and criminal time merge, and Lau receives dual compensation. Ngai Wing-hau, crime boss and Chan's half-brother, also enjoys taking his watch off to better appreciate the costs involved with the passage of time. For Ngai, time is cyclical, and he fondly quotes his father's favorite saying, "What goes around comes around."[28] He takes off the watch to mark time spent with his police interrogators while his minions kill off the competition and attempt to exact revenge for the death of Ngai's father. The watch marks both the time in the cycle for retribution and his power to control time to his advantage against the interests of the police as well as the other triads.

For Dr. Lee, time revolves around the alarm clock that marks the end of her sessions with Chan. Trying to avoid hypnosis that might undermine his cover, Chan uses a noisy, wind-up clock as a distraction. Eventually, professional time (i.e., time spent with a patient) merges with personal time (i.e., time spent with her lover). While Chan sleeps in her office, Lee plays solitaire — passing time — on the computer. Chan takes advantage of Lee's time, trying to negotiate between maintaining his cover, romancing the pretty doctor, and avoiding the jail time hanging over his head if he cannot successfully complete his anger management counseling.

In *Infernal Affairs III*, Lau literally steals Lee's time. When unknown criminals (actually Lau) break into her office, cash, watches, and the computer vanish. Obsessed with watches of all sorts, Lau clearly could not resist Lee's timepiece, even though the computer was his main objective. The watch — time — has moved outside of the rational world of gift, status symbol, measure of power, and marker of human intimacy into the irrational world of Lau's obsession — linked to Mary (Carina Lau) and her gold watch.

The stolen watches denote Lau's growing interest in Lee as he identifies with the deceased Chan.

The *Infernal Affairs* trilogy obsessively foregrounds narrative time. Covering 1991–2003, the films zero in on key moments repeatedly — the expulsion from the police academy, the triad initiation, Chan's death, the rooftop showdown, Billy's execution in the elevator, etc. The films also elide years and glide past the casting changes from the young Chan (Shawn Yue) and Lau (Edison Chen) to their older selves (Tony Leung, Andy Lau). *Infernal Affairs III* often vertiginously cuts between events in 2002 before Chan's death and events in 2003 following Lau and his descent into madness. While the handover figures prominently in *Infernal Affairs II*, other topical events from the period fade from view as the films spiral in on their own temporal orders. Bad timing (e.g., the botched drug deal and bust in *Infernal Affairs I*), missed appointments (e.g., Lau's failure to meet Mary to discuss their divorce in *Infernal Affairs III*), miscalculated time (e.g., May's hiding the identity of Chan's daughter by giving a younger age), and "forgotten time" (e.g., repressed memory) characterize the trilogy's depiction of time. In *Infernal Affairs I*, Wong and Sam match wits over time — Sam changing times and dates to avoid capture, and Wong trying to stay on top of his prey. In *Infernal Affairs II*, Wong and his colleague Superintendent Luk compete for busts and, conveniently, find it "difficult" to notify one another of changes in their operating schedule. *Infernal Affairs III* matches Lau's time pursuing Superintendent Yeung (Leon Lai) with Yeung's time trailing Lau.

Infernal Chronotopes: Time Takes on Flesh

In *The Dialogic Imagination*, Mikhail Bakhtin defines the term "chronotope" — a blending of "chronos" (time) and "topos" (space)

— that reflects his interest in the relative nature of time and space following Albert Einstein's concept of relativity in physics:

> The chronotope is where the knots of narrative are tied and untied ... Time becomes, in effect, palpable and visible; the chronotope makes narrative events concrete, makes them take on flesh, causes blood to flow in their veins.[29]

> Time, as it were, thickens, takes on flesh, becomes artistically visible; likewise, space becomes charged and responsive to the movements of time, plot and history.[30]

Of course, Bakhtin developed the notion of the chronotope at a time when the idea of temporality was coming under considerable scrutiny. With the disciplining of labor as a result of the industrial revolution and the rise of capitalism, Marx developed the notion of "surplus value" (i.e., labor time transformed into profit). Freud's concept of repression (i.e., the symptom as a consequence of events in the past), and Henri Bergson's investigations into time and memory as well as Martin Heidegger's[31] philosophical inquiries into time and being all show evidence of changing attitudes toward time. Time also takes on a concrete spatial dimension as hidden labor becomes the concrete commodity for Marx, repressed desires become visible symptoms for Freud, and time warps in relation to space for Einstein.

Even before the title of the film appears on screen, *Infernal Affairs II* self-consciously presents itself as a film about "time" and "space" by referring to the Buddhist hell alluded to in the Chinese title of the film: "Avici Hell. Also known as Continuous Hell. Uninterrupted time. Unlimited space." Although Bakhtin refers to literary genres in his discussion of the chronotope, the concept provides an approach to the distinct way each film in the *Infernal Affairs* trilogy concretizes time and space within the narrative.[32] Indeed, the way in which each film "interrupts" time and "limits" space highlights their differences.

In *Infernal Affairs I*, the chronotope of the *policier* dominates. The film focuses on the undercover operation of Chan within the triads and the world of police investigation associated with the mole Lau and Superintendent Wong. Time involves police procedures, tracking leads, communicating with informants. When the past intrudes (e.g., in Dr. Lee's questions during Chan's analysis, flashbacks to the police academy), it remains clearly marked in the plot and quickly suppressed. Space primarily involves the police station, the psychiatrist's office, the gangsters' meeting grounds, and the rooftops and other completely open "hiding places" in which Chan meets his handler Wong (Still 2.9).

Still 2.9   *Infernal Affairs:* roof

In *Infernal Affairs II*, a shift occurs, and the chronotope fleshes out the gangster genre's melodramatic sense of time and space. Time becomes more cyclical and ritualized according to the gangsters' laws of revenge and retribution. Space involves not only the gangsters' business enterprises, but domestic and semi-domestic spaces from palatial homes to triad haunts in restaurants, bars, and "martial arts associations." The triad style, associated with films and media reports from the 1990s, situates the film temporally with a mise-en-scène dominated by loud Hawaiian print shirts and oversized mobile phones. Covering the years from 1991 to 1997, the political time of Hong Kong's change of sovereignty becomes more salient, and Hong Kong as a specific place becomes more obvious. The city as a particular location in relation to Great Britain, China, and the rest of Asia, and its colonial history come into sharper focus.

Infernal Affairs III marks another shift in chronotope, and time and space become closely linked with what Fredric Jameson calls the "conspiratorial text":

> ... whatever other messages it emits or implies, may also be taken to constitute an unconscious, collective effort at trying to figure out where we are and what landscapes and forces confront us in a late twentieth century whose abominations are heightened by their concealment and their bureaucratic impersonality. Conspiracy film takes a wild stab at the heart of all that, in a situation in which it is the intent and the gesture that counts. Nothing is gained by having been persuaded of the definitive verisimilitude of this or that conspiratorial hypothesis: But in the intent to hypothesize, in the desire called cognitive mapping — therein lies the beginning of wisdom.[33]

Moving from the late twentieth to the early twenty-first century, the paranoia associated with the conspiratorial text still proves salient. Time revolves around surveillance, and space appears bounded by closed circuit television images.[34] Although the police moles wear wires when undercover in all three films, the level of surveillance within the police headquarters — the battle of the bug between Lau in Internal Affairs and Yeung in the Security Unit — takes the paranoia associated with seeing, being seen, discovering, and being discovered to a new level. Cramped offices, computer screens, and cyberspace replace the rooftops of *Infernal Affairs I* and the gangster haunts of *Infernal Affairs II*. With Lau's mental collapse, the "interior" time and space of the character's psyche also bleed out into the "exterior" pictorial realm of the diegesis. The slippery relationship between paranoid schizophrenia and the machinations of a malevolent, nearly omnipotent conspiratorial cabal become the basis for *Infernal Affairs III* and put it in conversation with films such as Michelangelo Antonioni's *Blow-Up* (1966), Brian De Palma's *Blow Out* (1981), and Francis Ford

Coppola's *The Conversation* (1974) in which the protagonists must confront the possibility that they are losing their sanity as they engage in surveillance.

Although the desire to create a "cognitive map" may be there (and, indeed, Lau's and Yeung's offices are filled with maps of all kinds), the implosion of the system at the film's bloody climax, does not, ultimately, resolve the problem of moles within the police force. Although the presence of Shen/Shadow may bring comfort to some as the Mainland figure of authority who remains above the fray, he, like a Hollywood Western hero, moves out of the picture at the end, leaving the Hong Kong force to make sense of and clean up the loose ends. Like Lau's mind, the social world of Hong Kong — its identity, political status, economic standing, etc. — remain muddled in relation to the shadowy presence of the People's Republic. Whether a conspiracy of triads (transnational corporate capitalism) or of government agents in league with Chinese operatives (the totalitarian nation-state) holds sway, the resultant paranoia remains palpable, and the picture painted of contemporary society bleak.

All three films repeat key times and places to present them from different perspectives, emphasizing different aspects of time and place within the story. *Infernal Affairs I* involves the breakdown of the rational time of the typical police story. Rather than leading to the discovery of the mole in the police force and the vindication of the police plant in the mob, the film ends with the death of the police officer and the celebration of the triad mole as a hero. Any sense of the just working of the police as representatives of the state disappears as Lau eliminates his triad boss, as well as threats of disclosure from his triad "brothers," and maintains his cover as a model cop. *Infernal Affairs II* does the same for the triads by eliminating any romantic celebration of the outlaw as a corrective to the corrupt state. The triad world implodes. Although Sam hangs on and becomes boss because he successfully manipulates his contacts in the police force, the "old" world of gangland "honor" represented by the Ngai family cannot make the transition from colonial Hong Kong to the SAR. *Infernal Affairs III* revolves around "interior" time and space; i.e., the inner world of Lau's mind, the inner workings of the police force, and the interior world of the television screen, computer monitor, and cell phone visual display.

All three films play with the tension between surface and depth, but in very different ways. In *Infernal Affairs I*, the surface cover cracks, and the moles' double lives become exposed. *Infernal Affairs II* revolves around the forces of history and the depth of traditions beneath the surface of change. *Infernal Affairs III* looks at psychological depth in relation to the rationality of the state and the criminal justice system.

To illuminate these differences, it may be useful to look at the single moment in the story that is reiterated in all three films — that is, Chan's expulsion from the police academy as Lau looks on. Although the moment remains identical in time (1991) and space (the police school), its signification shifts dramatically as it moves from one place in the narrative to another. Chan Wing-yan (Shawn Yue) walks out of the prison yard. Chan turns, Lau Kin-ming (Edison Chen) looks off-screen, and the editing appears to match the two characters' eye-lines. However, that apparent match may be deceptive. An off-screen voice narrates Chan's humiliating expulsion and asks if any cadet would like to trade places with him. In close-up, looking off-screen toward the camera, Lau whispers under his breath that he would trade places with Chan. The scene visually equates the two and places them literally on either side of the fence (one inside the school yard and one barred from it) as well as connected by their fleeting glance. Given that the information provided during the pre-credit sequence of the first film in the trilogy only shows Lau's initiation into the triads as a police mole and Chan's successful test to become an undercover cop, Lau's wish to change places seems to exhibit his dissatisfaction with the life of a police cadet and Chan's apparently uncomplicated choice to become an informer. A black-and-white freeze frame isolates Lau and fixes him in this moment like a photographic document of his state at that point in time (Still 2.10). However, the narrative does not fix the meaning of the scene in the same way the visual seems to point to a frozen, captured, unchanging moment in time.

Still 2.10   *Infernal Affairs:* young Lau at police academy

While the pre-credit sequence moves to fix Lau's identity, Chan becomes the first to voice his identity crisis in the film. Flashbacks to the academy intrude as he tells Superintendent Wong that he wants out. He has difficulty controlling his violent outbursts, and he cannot keep his cover while maintaining the behavior appropriate to his job as a police officer. At the end of the film, Chan's turn and apparent eye-line match with Lau returns, but Tony Leung and Andy Lau have replaced Shawn Yue and Edison Chen (Stills 2.11 and 2.12). Now, at the film's conclusion, after several murders to maintain his identity as a police officer, Lau's desire to trade places with Chan takes on a completely different significance. Instead of desiring to be free of the academy to be a "real" gangster, he seems to want to be a "real" cop (even dead) rather than an ersatz officer constantly threatened with exposure. Of course, ironically, his desire to be "good" has led him to be the most villainous character in the film — killing or leading to the deaths of nearly all the major characters. As the actors switch to occupy the same roles, identities can no longer be photographically fixed by a frozen black and white close shot. Rather, the concluding scene in *Infernal Affairs I* places its principals' identities in flux by highlighting Lau's "true" desire to be a cop rather than a crook. Chan can smugly leave the academy behind, since his identity as a cop has been confirmed after his death, but Lau's desire to trade places with him seems to point to a continuing dissatisfaction with his place within the police force. He has not been exposed, but he would still rather be dead (Chan) than alive and thriving as a police hero who managed to kill triad kingpin Sam and Billy, the mole who killed Chan. Authenticity seems to mean more to Lau than confirmed — if fleeting — success.

Still 2.11 *Infernal Affairs:* Lau goes from young to old at police academy

Still 2.12 *Infernal Affairs:* Chan turns at police academy

Infernal Affairs II complicates this moment further. Chan (Shawn Yue) and Lau (Edison Chen) again appear to exchange glances. However, this moment now occurs in a different context. Lau has killed Chan's father, Kwun, and Kwun's wish to have his estranged son Chan informed of his passing has exposed the police cadet as the son of a mobster. Rather than agreeing to become a mole because of Wong's recognition of his talents as an officer in training (e.g., his ability to observe and notice Wong's mismatched socks), Chan actually has been singled out because of his blood kinship with the triads. In fact, he has little choice in the matter. Whether he agrees to become an informer or not, he cannot continue his police training. The fact he hid his family crime connections automatically disqualifies him, so his only way to maintain his coveted identity as a "cop" is to become a member of the triads (Still 2.13).

Still 2.13   *Infernal Affairs II:* Chan leaves police academy

The moment changes in relation to Lau as well. If the first iteration indicates a desire to be outside the force in order to be free to be a gangster and the second implies a desire to be an authentic cop in order to maintain his marriage to Mary and respectable profession and bourgeois household, then the third iteration points to a further complication. As a murderer, his identity has been inexorably fixed. If, at first, Lau may have been able to change his identity and destiny — at least in the eyes of his wife Mary or the film viewers — that possibility, in retrospect, never existed. In this version, Lau's identity and fate appear to be sealed by the murder of Kwun. The police academy becomes not only an entry into the world of the mole, but, also, the ideal hideout for a killer on the run from the authorities. If *Infernal Affairs I* follows the *policier*'s chronotope of investigation, discovery, and possibility, then *Infernal Affairs II* fixes its characters' destinies following what Robert Warshow has called the "tragedy" of the gangster genre.[35]

Also, in this iteration of the scene, the historical context of the cadet's training becomes more significant. Before Chan's exposure as Kwun's son, Chan had been dining with his superiors as they discussed the 1997 handover and its consequences. The limitations of the possibilities the narrative held for these characters in the scene as shown in *Infernal Affairs II* further narrow, but, historically, their identities become complicated by the change in sovereignty of Hong Kong. The scene has taken away the possibility that Chan could remain in the academy and made it less likely (even though Mary had offered to talk to Sam about Lau's situation) for Lau, the murderer, to walk away from the relative safety of the training school. Their moral identities may be less in question; i.e., Chan's willingness to go undercover in order to maintain his dream of being "good" and Lau's inability to put the "bad" world of the triads behind him. However, 1997 has complicated the matter again by putting another aspect of the characters' identity in question as they transform themselves from colonial subjects to Chinese nationals.

Later in the film, this question of identity, morality, and state power resurfaces when the fact that Wong conspired with Mary to kill Kwun emerges. Indirectly, Lau, when he murdered Kwun, worked for the state — albeit, illegally and "unofficially" — in the person of SP Wong. Without knowing it, Lau acted as a cop, under orders from a cop. Chan's and Lau's identities again become unhinged. The meaning of their supposedly "fixed" identities as cop and crook has become much less certain as the status of the state and the rule of law become less certain.[36] Ironically, although narrative possibilities have been dramatically closed off by the new information, the status of the characters' identities has become even more malleable. This exacerbates their "tragic" fates — Lau as victim of Mary and Wong's manipulation and Chan as subject to the inflexible rules of the police force and the machinations of Wong.

In *Infernal Affairs III*, the moment returns as Lau slips into madness. Lau goes to his clothes closet. Flashbacks of Chan's eyes — associated with Chan and Lau's final fateful meeting on the roof — merge into images of the young Chan turning into the older Chan as he turns to look behind him, through the gate of the police academy, at the time of his expulsion. Lau opens the door of the closet and sees Chan (Tony Leung) reflected back. This time the eye-line match marks a moment of recognition/misrecognition (reminiscent of Jacques Lacan's "mirror phase") as Lau begins to take on Chan's identity — rather than simply whispering his desire to trade places. Lau smiles at his reflection as Chan — and Chan smiles back (Still 2.14). In this version, the scruffy and unshaven Chan from *Infernal Affairs I* has cleaned up, and, clean shaven, presents a fitting ideal image of a cop for the delusional Lau (Still 2.15).

Still 2.14   *Infernal Affairs III:* Lau smiles back at Chan in mirror

Still 2.15   *Infernal Affairs III:* Chan looks at Lau

However, the duality of the moment is finally broken with the next iteration of the scene. Again, the young Lau becomes the older Lau, but, this time, the moment continues as Superintendent Yeung goes from younger to older (Leon Lai) and an off-screen voice reminds Yeung that he would not be the leading cadet in the academy if Chan had not been expelled. The younger Chan turns into the older Chan, turns back to look through the school gate, and winks. The dyadic intensity of the Chan/Lau dynamic has been broken by the introduction of Yeung as a third witness. However, this moment in time is filtered through Shen/"Shadow"'s recollection of something Yeung told him that Shen repeats for Dr.

Lee's benefit. The moment fractures again — from the extreme subjective intensity of Lau's misrecognition of himself as Chan to the distance of a recollection of someone else's reminiscence. Although it gains narrative depth, the moment recedes into layers of mediation that drain it of the immediacy it had when first presented in the trilogy. These extremes fit in well with the chronotope associated with the conspiracy film — constantly under surveillance, self-perception becomes more problematic and focus shifts from the principals to others who may not have seemed significant earlier.

In each iteration of the moment, time and space are fixed, but the instant of recollection changes from flashbacks associated with a specific character's memory (e.g., Chan on the roof with Wong), a specific character's fantasy (e.g., Lau in front of the mirror), a character's recollection of another's memory (e.g., Shen recalls Yeung's version), or with the moment presented within a different sequence of events — achronologically — without being marked by a particular character's subjectivity (e.g., the first version and its final reiteration in *Infernal Affairs I* and its presentation in *Infernal Affairs II*). Time and space do not fix memory, identity, morality, or history. Rather, the moment marks a crisis in time and space in relation to cinematic narrative. Presumably, the moment could be repeated ad infinitum and always be different — representing a different chronotope, but, also, paradoxically, absolutely fixed in time and space. The moment illustrates the break between classical notions of storytelling and what could be termed a "postmodern" approach.

At the end of *Cinema I: The Movement-Image* and the beginning of *Cinema II: The Time-Image*, Gilles Deleuze talks about a crisis in the "movement-image" (i.e., the certainty of narratives subordinating time to movement in space including — but not limited to — classical Hollywood cinema) that can be seen emerging in a number of films from *Citizen Kane* (1941) and Hitchcock's

Hollywood films through Italian Neo-Realism, the French New Wave, New American Cinema, New German Cinema, and beyond. Without quite making the transition to what Deleuze would call the "direct image of time" of the "time-image," these transitional or "crisis" films point toward the latter. Characters become "seers" rather than actors. Thought and memory replace action.[37] Space becomes disconnected, fragmented, and autonomous from the plot. The relation between action and setting becomes dreamlike and disjointed. Relations — between characters, actions, times, or places — become difficult to determine.

The *Infernal Affairs* trilogy seems to fit the bill. Although linked to action genres (e.g., police stories, gangster films), the films' directors themselves note that *Infernal Affairs* lacks "action." A great deal of the films' narrative time revolves around listening (e.g., the scene in the stereo store) and watching (e.g., the glances exchanged — or not — at the police academy). Car garages, concrete rooftops, convenience stores, office complexes, and the sterile, institutional settings of hospitals and police stations provide the anonymous, disconnected spaces for much of the trilogy. These spaces mirror Hong Kong as a city as its identity changes with its sovereignty.

The Infernal City: Space and Non-Place

> ... for the gangster there is only the city; he must inhabit it in order to personify it: not the real city, but that dangerous and sad city of the imagination which is so much more important, which is the modern world. And the gangster — though there are real gangsters — is also, and primarily, a creature of the imagination. The real city, one might say, produces only criminals; the imaginary city produces the gangster: he is what we want to be and what we are afraid we may become.
>
> — Robert Warshow, "The Gangster as Tragic Hero," 1948[38]

Yingchi Chu sees a marked change after 1997 in the depiction of Hong Kong in the cinema:

> Fear and depression are shown in the portrayal of the Hong Kong landscape .... . Hong Kong's skyscrapers and shopping centres are presented as sites for potential dangers threatening unexpectedly and suddenly in elevators, air-conditioned tunnels, nearby streets and parking areas. In contrast to the 1980s .... . Hong Kong's pride in its modern buildings and confidence in the control of its technology are absent in the post-1997 films.[39]

Infernal Affairs provides a complex image of post-1997 Hong Kong as a "city of the imagination." Hong Kong serves as both a specific place with a specific history, dating back to prehistoric settlements along its coasts, and as an emblem of the "global" city,[40] one among many postmodern urban centers that share common architectural designs, cosmopolitan populations, transnational commercial structures, and economic bases in finance, merchandising, design, service, and communication industries (Still 2.16). While traces of the traditional Chinese marketplace, the colonial port, and the neo-colonial center of light industry/small-scale manufacturing remain,

Still 2.16 *Infernal Affairs:* market

Hong Kong as a postmodern metropolis moves beyond these places into the transnational and transitory realm of the "non-place."

In *Infernal Affairs*, this means the domination of the "non-place" within the mise-en-scène. As Marc Augé, in conversation with the work of Michel de Certeau, describes it:

> ... non-places are the real measure of our time; one that could be quantified — with the aid of a few conversions between area, volume and distance — by totaling all the air, rail and motorway routes, the mobile cabins called "means of transport" (aircraft, trains and road vehicles), the airports and railway stations, hotel chains, leisure parks, large retail outlets, and finally the complex skein of cable and wireless networks that mobilize extraterrestrial space of the purposes of communication so peculiar that it often puts the individual in contact only with another image of himself.[41]

Although "places" like Ngai's home play an important role in the trilogy, non-places (or, "places" transformed into "non-places) come to dominate. Rooftops, parking garages, convenience stores, bank branches, and multiplex cinemas serve as temporary meeting sites or drops for information. These non-places could be anywhere in the world, and they bear few, if any markers, of Hong Kong as a city or even Asia as a region.

Lau's apartment he so carefully decorates with Mary has a similar impersonality and homogenized blandness — as if it just emerged from the Ikea warehouse (Still 2.17). Moreover, Lau never gets to settle completely into his apartment, which functions as a

Still 2.17   *Infernal Affairs:* Lau at home

"non-place" of transition. Even the solidity of the police station dissolves as it becomes wired and rewired for surveillance and the transfer of information. Other than the exterior shots that mark specific police stations, the interior of the stations consist of generic office furniture, partitions, computers, telephones, and audiovisual displays. Only the specifics of the streets projected onto the office white boards offer any indication that the fluorescent lights and mini-Venetian blinds of the interior spaces actually open out to the city of Hong Kong. Characters spend considerable time in airport and hospital waiting rooms, hotel rooms, convenience stores, on the telephone/cell phone, lost in the cyberspace of the computer screen or CCTV monitor, in cars or on the subway, in parking garages, or other "non-places" that emphasize their postmodern deterritorialization (Stills 2.18, 2.19, 2.20). The mise-en-scène captures characters within these "non-places" as ephemeral images reflected in television or computer monitors or blurred figures on the skin of glass skyscrapers (Still 2.21).[42]

Still 2.18 *Infernal Affairs III:* hospital waiting room

Still 2.19 *Infernal Affairs III:* Wong and Chan in 7-Eleven

Still 2.20 *Infernal Affairs:* parking garage

Still 2.21 *Infernal Affairs:* reflection in window

The rooftops of office buildings provide particularly important spaces in *Infernal Affairs I* and *III* as realms separate from the quotidian workings of the city, above the business being conducted on the floors below, as well as privileged vantage points for surveying the Hong Kong cityscape and, thus, being at the very heart of the urban center (Still 2.22). Not only does Chan meet and bond with his mentor Wong on rooftops, Lau also becomes part of the inner circle within the police department when he meets with his superiors practicing their golf swing on the roof of police headquarters. The roof offers a sense of solidity, of being in charge of all that can be seen, and, simultaneously, of danger, the fear of falling, and the anxiety of meeting with the higher-ups who might find an underling wanting.

Still 2.22 *Infernal Affairs:* Chan on roof with cell phone

A long history exists of rooftops in the cinema, which includes King Kong's assault on New York City, its parody in Peter Mak's *Wicked City* (1992), Scottie (Jimmy Stewart) on the roof in *Vertigo* (1958), Howard Roark (Gary Cooper) in *The Fountainhead* (1949), as well as the psychotic Cody Jarrett (James Cagney) declaring he has made it to the "top of the world" in *White Heat* (1949), another undercover cop story with Edmond O'Brien as the mole. Hong Kong crime films feature many memorable rooftop scenes as well, including the tops of skyscrapers in several films by Johnnie To and Wai Ka-fai, among others. The rooftop is a liminal space, barely visible from the street and not seen from the interior. It marks where the sky meets the human construction of the building, and it becomes a fitting threshold to explore other limits. Although speaking of the cinematic skyline of Taipei, Zhang Yingjin's description also holds true of Hong Kong seen from above in *Infernal Affairs*:

> ... the landscape from above, at once rendering a breathtaking feeling of superiority, a titillating *jouissance* of voyeurism, and the effect of complete distanciation and defamiliarization between the viewer and the city ... a representation, an optical artifact, a visual simulacrum.[43]

For Chan, a model of urban angst and alienation, the rooftop is where he feels free to express his emotions to SP Wong, unburdening himself, revealing his neurosis, intimating he fears he will lose his mind if he remains undercover. For Lau, the rooftop becomes the imaginative space in which his psychosis takes shape as he replays the moments leading up to Chan's murder in a way that absolves him of responsibility in *Infernal Affairs III* (Still 2.23). The rooftop, too, again drawing on film history, becomes the arena in which the drama reaches its climax and the final confrontation between the protagonist and antagonist takes place (Still 2.24). It is the end point — the highest point that can be attained before the protagonist falls to earth — and it promises the possibility of redemption (heaven) or the inevitability of a fall (hell) — and, indeed, SP Wong's fall to his death provides one of the more dramatic moments in *Infernal Affairs I* (Still 2.25).

Still 2.23   *Infernal Affairs III:* Lau's flashback

Still 2.24   *Infernal Affairs:* Lau and Chan face off on roof

Still 2.25   *Infernal Affairs:* Wong
dead on taxi

However, the rooftop also represents the border between the
non-place of the anonymous, urban environment (Still 2.26) and
the cityscape of Hong Kong that references its history of trade (the
harbor dotted with container ships) (Still 2.27), class divisions (the
colonial elite on the Peak), and bid to play an indispensable role in
the world economy (structures like the Bank of China and HSBC
buildings) (Still 2.28). From the rooftops, too, the cityscape's
identity also becomes problematic as monuments to the PRC's
investment in Hong Kong, like the Bank of China, loom over the
machinations of Ngai and the informer Chan. The bland emptiness
of the rooftops — dotted with ventilation pipes and barriers — vies
with glimpses of the city beyond to provide the vertiginous backdrop
for the climax of *Infernal Affairs I*. The rooftop mirrors the
psychological issues of identity Chan and Lau encounter as

essentially anonymous cogs in the machinery of transnational capitalism managed by the state or as embodiments of a specific local identity associated with Hong Kong triads and the Hong Kong police.

Still 2.26 *Infernal Affairs:* roof pipes

Still 2.27 *Infernal Affairs:* rooftop view

Still 2.28 *Infernal Affairs II:* Chan and Ngai with Bank of China

In fact, the trilogy plays with the tensions between the global and the local throughout as it moves from the specifics of places that have become tourist haunts (the Lantau Buddha, Jumbo Floating Restaurant) or typify Hong Kong of an earlier era (e.g., *dai pai dong*, hot pot bistros, sidewalk religious shrines, shacks in the New Territories) to the unmarked spaces of global consumer culture from the convenience store to the office building. Sam dreams of moving out of the backwaters of the New Territories and the second-class status associated with Kowloon into Central, the urban heart of Hong Kong Island. Urban space marks global desires from the nondescript furniture in Lau's apartment to billboard advertisements for Hollywood films. It also collapses time as colonial holdovers continue to form the skyline of the SAR.

Rooftops are the haunts of those who have no place in the buildings or on the streets below. Aside from the occasional workman, they provide a space for the criminal, the deviant, and the vagrant. In addition, rooftops represent spaces forbidden to the uninitiated and off-limits to the general population. They are taboo, and, perhaps because of this, take on a libidinal significance. The rooftop provides a quintessential male perch on top of phallic protuberances, and it seems fitting moments of doubt surrounding identity and male authority should be played out on the roofs of Hong Kong. Chan comes down to earth as a corpse in an elevator (Still 2.29), and Wong hurtles down from the heights to land dead on a taxi. Lau ends up outside the city entirely in the bucolic setting of the sanitarium — sandwiched between the two Marys whom he crossed — outside of the cityscape he dominated as a gangster.[44] In fact, the police graveyard featured in the trilogy provides an elevated space, with a view of the city beyond, which brings the rooftops and the hospital lawn together in a place associated with death, memory, and the transition from British colonialism to PRC rule symbolized by the flags that flutter over the graves.

Still 2.29   *Infernal Affairs:* Chan dead in elevator

Between the exposed rooftop and the cemetery, the womblike stereo store provides a privileged space of rest and security in the world of consumerism. Away from the bustle of the streets and the overwhelming immensity of the shopping mall, the stereo store privileges a world of small scale capitalism, where buyer and seller can meet as fellows and bond around a music system and a packaged, seductive voice. While the rooftop represents the pinnacle of global capitalism bringing the flows of commerce into the solidity of the office building, the stereo store, hidden away on a nondescript street, speaks to another moment in Hong Kong's economic history — the transnational economy under wraps and out of the way, the place of real desire. Whether watching *Infernal Affairs* in a multiplex in Hong Kong or on a home video system in the United States or Europe, the stereo store offers a comforting, nostalgic vision of mass culture. Like Tsai Chin, *Infernal Affairs* offers specialized enjoyment to the initiated abroad and a homey familiarity to the local audience weaned on triad stories.

While the rooftop signifies crisis and hubris, the stereo store presents a more comforting version of capitalism at ease with technology, identity, and memory. As Lau shops for a stereo to build up his domestic space, the store takes on the trappings of home. The stereo store seems to take a page out of Jane Jacobs's book in which she laments massive, impersonal, corporate office towers driving small businesses out of the city.[45] Although she analyzes the American city, her remarks echo Hong Kong's own celebration of the small entrepreneur, the "boss" of his own establishment, and the values of the family business. The rich and the working classes disappear, and the "yuppie" emerges as "boss" and consumer, merchant and bureaucrat (i.e., Lau never plays the role of "working class" cop).

With an environment that hints at nostalgia, memory, repression, desire, technology, and identity, the stereo store encapsulates the "imaginary community" that has taken the place of the "imagined community" of Hong Kong.[46] Ackbar Abbas notes:

... the space of Hong Kong is a space of "uneven development" in a specific sense: it is a space traversed by different times and speeds, where change has no clear direction but is experienced as a series of anticipations and residues that jostle each other for position ... the city dealt with dependency by developing a tendency toward timelessness ... and placelessness ... a tendency to live its own version of the "floating world" without the need to establish stable identities.[47]

As such, Hong Kong exemplifies David Harvey's formulation of the postmodern city as "theatre, a series of stages upon which individuals could work their own distinctive magic while performing a multiplicity of roles."[48] On the roof, Chan/Tony Leung and Lau/Andy Lau become actors/stars/ "monuments" within the same cityscape as the buildings that define Hong Kong. As stars, they represent Hong Kong to the world. Larger than life on screen they take on the monumentality of the buildings against which they are framed. However, ultimately, they also represent the city as "theatre," and their identities as stars become subject to passing fashions, ephemeral and without depth. Thus, their destabilized identities as star images embodied by actors playing the roles of moles become part of the postmodern "placelessness" of the staged backdrop of Hong Kong as an urban image. On the rooftops of office buildings or in the shops of small businesses, the characters in *Infernal Affairs* operate in the "any-space-whatever" of global cinema that Mark Shiel, drawing on Gilles Deleuze, describes as: "... a space in which the intangibility of global capitalism is particularly apparent."[49] Cinematic space becomes commodified through the fetishized image of the city.

3

Allegories of Hell:
Moral Tales and National Shadows

Given the space in Hong Kong films mirrors the "uneven development" of the city itself, the mise-en-scène of *Infernal Affairs* includes spaces associated with the traditional (e.g., 10,000 Buddha Temple), the modern (e.g., colonial-era buildings), and the postmodern (e.g., the mélange of non-places within the urban fabric of Hong Kong). Likewise, *Infernal Affairs* presents a story that includes layers attached to traditional preoccupations with Buddhism, Confucianism, clan loyalties, and patriarchal prerogatives, to questions of colonialism/post-colonialism and the issue of "national" identity, and to postmodern preoccupations with the transnational, post-industrial economy, consumerism, and the information society. *Infernal Affairs* narrates different versions of these "stories." Thus, the trilogy opens up to multiple allegorical readings that co-exist within the narrative — occasionally contradicting one another, supporting one another, or canceling each other out.

Buddhism and Fate

Infernal Affairs' title in English and Chinese refers to the infernal, and the tribulations of Buddhist hell place the film within the realm of religious allegory.[1] Like Dante's *Inferno*, the trilogy links the contemporary world with the punishments of hell to proffer a cautionary moral tale. *Infernal Affairs I* begins with reference to a Buddhist sutra: "The worst of the eight hells is continuous hell — it has the meaning of continuous suffering." It ends with: "Says the Buddha: He who is in Continuous Hell never dies. Longevity is a big hardship in Continuous Hell." *Infernal Affairs II* ends with the title: "Continuous hell embodies 3 components: Uninterrupted time. Unlimited space. Boundless suffering. Transgressors of the five deadly sins fall into this hell forever — condemned to the ultimate incessant suffering." *Infernal Affairs III* ends with: "People of the like shall be cast into the Avici Hell and will continue to suffer from Kalpas to Kalpas with no means of escape." The way that leads to "no where" ("wu jian") in the trilogy's Chinese title *Wu Jian Dao* (Cantonese: *Mou Gaan Dou*) does not refer to an empty space; rather, "no space" means a limitless space and a continuous time filled with suffering. "Kalpas" refer to the millennial cycles that the sinner must spend in hell. The cycle of suffering includes repeated deaths, resurrections, suffering, and more death. Thus, "longevity is a hardship," because the soul cannot be released to continue its cycle of reincarnation in order to improve its karma. The soul remains stuck in time and space — unable to move on. The transgressions that lead to this hell include disregard for filial duties (particularly killing or harming one's parents) and various types of sacrilege (desecration of Buddhist shrines, impersonating holy men, etc.)

The characters in *Infernal Affairs* provide an apt illustration of this concept of hell. They become stuck in time and space — unable to move on and unable to stay put. Buddhist symbols appear repeatedly in the film, and characters refer to sayings about karma repeatedly (e.g., "what goes around comes around," "men don't change events, events change men," "there is no present without the past," etc.) The trilogy begins with the camera moving vertiginously around an image of Buddha, and the first scene takes place in Shatin's famous Temple of 10,000 Buddhas in Hong Kong's New Territories (Still 3.1). Sam bows to an image of Buddha before he instructs his recruits about his plans to infiltrate the Hong Kong police. He sees himself as a Caesar-like figure and his underlings as expendable in his quest for power. They drink as a sign of their obedience. In Buddhism, the root of all evil is desire, and Sam seems filled with ambition. Bringing his quest for power through subversion of the police to a temple seems absolutely antithetical to Buddhist doctrine, blasphemous, and reason enough to be cast into Avici hell.

Still 3.1 *Infernal Affairs:* 10,000 Buddhas

However, the vastness of "continuous time" and "unlimited space" proves large enough to contain contradictions. Sam states in *Infernal Affairs III*, "I am a real triad." Although characters discuss their identities (e.g., "cops," "good guys," and "bad guys") throughout the trilogy, only Sam owns up to being a "real triad." Of course, this means that Sam traces his roots back to the burning of the Southern Shaolin Temple during the Qing Dynasty (under Manchu Emperors) and the scattering of loyalists who formed secret societies in order to attempt to restore Ming (ethnic Han) rule. Underground, looking for ways to finance their cause, many of these triads branched out into other illegal activities. Although organizations as diverse as Sun Yat-sen's Nationalist party and many martial arts schools can trace their roots to this anti-Qing movement and the legendary destruction of the Shaolin Temple, criminal triads use their history in connection with Buddhist-based resistance to Qing rule as a way to legitimate their criminal activities.[2] Sam stands in a Buddhist temple as a general going to battle against an "illegitimate" state — i.e., perhaps not the Qings, but the British colonial government. Rather than personal desire, he represents a just — but criminal — war on the state. Sam's underlings can be assured that they are part of a larger and justifiable plan that gives meaning to their lives and deaths within the underworld. As a triad and as a Buddhist, Sam takes his chances standing in front of his new troops under the gaze of more than 10,000 Buddhas.

The relationship between chance and fate operates as an important motif in the trilogy. Superintendent Wong uses playing cards as a metaphor for his relationship with Sam in *Infernal Affairs I*, and the cards return in concrete form as a "fixed" pack of cards Wong uses to get his way with Superintendent Luk. Gradually, the characters come to understand that all the decks are "stacked" and that they already know what hands have been dealt. Although Dr. Lee modernizes the card game by playing on her computer, her game of solitaire does not give her any added control over the mechanism of fate. Within the Buddhist allegory, all the characters acquiesce to a fate, to the workings of karma, which they can never fully understand. Near the end of *Infernal Affairs II*, Sam remarks to Wong: "Retribution knows its own time. Who knows how you and I will end up?"

Sam's and Wong's fates, indeed, are intertwined. Even though Sam refuses to help Wong get rid of the triad boss Ngai Kwun, Wong, with the help of Sam's wife Mary and Lau, manages to eliminate Kwun and set Sam against the entire Ngai family. In fact, Sam discovers that he has been targeted while on a trip to Thailand. Predominantly Buddhist, Thailand often serves in Hong Kong film (and within the Greater Chinese imagination) as a wellspring of spirituality; impoverished, but holy, it stands in sharp contrast to materialist Hong Kong. Although Sam has been sent to Thailand on "business," the "business" at hand has nothing to do with commerce; rather, he has arrived there to meet his fate. Beginning with a golden Buddhist temple in the background, the camera follows Sam into a shrine in which he has been scheduled to meet his contact (actually his executioner). Sam smiles, bows, and rapidly picks up a knife to kill the man who has laid a trap for him. If Avici hell punishes those who desecrate Buddhist shrines, again, Sam appears to be an apt candidate, since he slaughters his enemies in a holy shrine and sets fire to a temple.

The Thai connection brings the karmic cycles to the foreground in *Infernal Affairs II*. Sam repeats the same offer that Wong had given him with Paul, the Thai gangster he had used as a shield to escape the temple. Sam proposes to help eliminate the Thai boss, so Paul can take command. To show his sincerity, Sam puts his loaded gun on the table between them. Keung begs Sam not to take the chance, but Sam goes through with it and gets shot in the chest. However, Sam survives, but his survival, ironically, leads to his wife Mary's death. Desperate to get away from Lau to help Sam, Mary repulses Lau's advances, and Lau, in turn, sets Mary up to be killed by Ngai's gang.

However, Mary's death also leads to retribution. At a beach in Thailand, Sam talks to Wong about having a Buddhist funeral for Mary. The monks promised that Mary could attain "eternal peace" if the living could stay with the body a bit longer after the chanting had ended. Since the body was not in the coffin, Sam became upset, but the monk comforted him by saying Mary was here — placing his hand on Sam's chest. Sam noted that the spot the monk touched was exactly where the Thai had shot him, and, again, Sam seems fated to avenge her death. Echoing Mary, he says, "I've passed the point of no return." In fact, Sam risks his life to manipulate the police into killing Ngai.

Although it remains unclear whether Sam blames Wong for manipulating Mary into arranging Kwun's death or whether he suspects Mary and Wong had an affair, Sam and Wong's collective history of involvement with Mary affects possible interpretations of *Infernal Affairs I* and *III*. After Ngai's death, Wong and Sam square off again as their mole avatars wreak havoc in each other's camp. Paul, the Thai gangster who shot Sam, becomes his business partner and slaughters Ngai's entire family. Paul reminds Sam that "you can never go too far." Given the unlimited nature of hell, this proves true. As an instrument of vengeance and undisputed crime boss, Sam descends further into a moral abyss.

Visually, the favored means of execution in the trilogy — a bullet through the middle of the forehead — parallels the Buddhist concept of the "third eye." In traditional Buddhist iconography, the third eye represents the "all seeing" nature of Buddha's enlightenment. Indeed, at the moment the bullets pierce their heads, the victims each attain a knowledge that had eluded them — which, in fact, has led to their deaths. Chan realizes that Lau is not the only mole, Billy discovers that Lau is willing to betray his gangster "brother," Sam discerns that Lau prefers the life of a cop to being his underling, Kwun sees that he has not safeguarded himself against his enemies, Ngai learns that his half-brother is a police mole, Yeung finds out that Lau has been confirmed as the mole, etc. However, this enlightenment comes too late, and none of these characters can escape fate. Buddhists believe that ignorance leads to suffering, and the nature of these executions underscores that point.

Echoing the opening of the first film in the trilogy, *Infernal Affairs III* also features a famous Buddhist site in Hong Kong. The camera looks up from a low angle on the giant Buddha of Lantau Island (Still 3.2). Sam burns incense and bows, while Liang, a Mainlander, speaking Mandarin, gives him a "lesson" in the PRC approach to doing business. Wanting to move in on Sam's business, Liang says: "We'll ask no questions. It's one country, two systems.

As long as money breeds money, we'll let you run the show. You think a Hong Kong triad can outlive a Mainland businessman?" Liang's brother, Shen, enters into the conversation by recognizing Sam as a Buddhist. Ingratiating himself, Shen asks about the *feng shui* of the spot and says he wants a commemorative tablet for himself and his wife to be placed there. Given that Sam has also lost his wife and holds Buddhist funerary practices in high regard, he pays close attention to Shen's wish and offers to handle it for him. They part laughing and shaking hands.

Still 3.2   *Infernal Affairs III:* Lantau Buddha

However, throughout the trilogy, a pattern has been established between Sam's joviality and his dangerousness. For example, he laughed with his Thai host before killing him at another shrine. Therefore, when Sam gives the assignment to look after the Mainlanders to Keung, who wants no part of it because he will likely bungle it, it underscores Sam's suspicions regarding his new business contacts. The "real" triad is suspicious of the outsider — even if they share a common religious and cultural tradition. The scene ends with a canted shot of the Buddha as clouds roll by. Part tourist attraction, part pilgrimage site, the Buddha on Lantau, like Sam and Shen, contains contradictions that cannot be reconciled — the spiritual and the material, the "real" triad and the "businessman," Hong Kong and the PRC, surface compliance and deep resistance.

Although Shen, actually an undercover cop from the PRC, may be tempting fate (and a stint in the Avici hell) by using Buddhism to insinuate himself into Sam's affairs in order to arrest him, the other sins that lead to Avici hell also play a role in the moral tale *Infernal Affairs* tells. Highlighting a moral directive that strikes a chord with Confucians as well as Buddhists, the worst punishment has been reserved for those who do not demonstrate filial piety and who, in fact, do harm to their forbearers.

Confucianism and Patriarchal Power

Buddhism operates within a moral universe that links human suffering to illusion, ignorance, and desire. Transgressions must be expunged, through the working of fate, in order for the soul to move on to attain enlightenment and end the cycle of suffering, death, and reincarnation. More worldly, Confucianism lays out the rules that govern correct behavior. Confucius's *Analects* point out how to behave properly toward superiors, inferiors, and equals. As Confucian thought developed in China, it took the patriarchal family as a model for all social relations with the exercise of power in the state modeled on the father's exercise of power over his household. Virtue depends on the smooth operation of this order. In *Infernal Affairs*, the operations of the police force as well as the triads rely on these Confucian principles that celebrate filial piety and male camaraderie. Rituals serve to concretize these values. When Chan enters the triads, he bows to a statue of Guan Gong — a famous general immortalized in *The Romance of the Three Kingdoms* and revered as the divine ancestor of both the police and triads. In fact, as a figure of war, he watches over all those who use blades in their professions — including cooks, etc. — and Chan's bowing to his effigy places him in an order within the triads that does not contradict his calling to be a cop (Still 3.3).[3]

In this world out of whack with the spirit of Confucianism, Chan and Lau find themselves very good at their respective professions, if not always happy about being moles. In *Infernal*

Still 3.3 *Infernal Affairs:* Guan Gong

Affairs II, before he leaves the police force, Chan has already proved himself on the streets as an enforcer by beating up Keung, whom he caught trying to steal a car. As cop and/or crook, he relishes the physical expression of his rage. In jail, he beats up his cellmate and, during a drug deal, he roughs up one of the Ngai family underlings. In *Infernal Affairs III,* Chan destroys a massage parlor under orders from Keung and attacks Shen's brother Liang with an ashtray under orders from Sam. Although Ngai, Keung, and his police handler Wong all complain that Chan goes too far, as a criminal, Chan can do what he would do as a cop in any case; i.e., beat up the gangsters.

In its picture of interlocked destinies, *Infernal Affairs* underscores that the triads and the police share the same goals; albeit, for very different reasons. Early in *Infernal Affairs I,* Lau, pretending to be an attorney, uses intelligence from Sam to triangulate on a drug deal eliminating Sam's competition. Also, Lau benefits, as both cop and crook, from assassinating Sam. Eliminating a criminal kingpin brings accolades to the cop and promotion to the gangster. In *Infernal Affairs III,* the police beat Chan to near unconsciousness after his attack on Liang — saving Sam, Shen, or Liang some of the trouble. Similarly, Wong tries to advance Sam's career because the underling may be easier to control than Kwun. Both sides benefit from a narrowing of the competition due to intimacy with the opponent, and each side can use the other to do its dirty work. Police break the law in order to enforce the law, and criminals cooperate with law enforcement in order to run their operations more profitably.

Of course, this complicates the Confucian order — since the interests of various figures of authority collide, and, although the state has official legitimacy on its side, it often fails to exercise moral authority. Even when beaten and left to rot, Chan, for example, has a confidence in the benevolence of the state that borders on blindness. In his insane attempt to solidify his identity as a police officer, Lau operates with that same blind confidence. Just as Wong and Sam find themselves on the same side as they go against Ngai, Chan and Lau share a common desire to be "legitimate," to be seen publicly as representatives of the state within the police force.

Infernal Affairs II begins with a scene in which Sam and Wong discuss the meaning of being "decent" or "good guys" — "hou yahn" (in Cantonese), "hao ren" (in Mandarin). Wong describes his first arrest in December 1980. One of Ngai Kwun's young thugs stabs his partner to death before Wong can draw his gun. Wong empties his gun into the murderer, but does not kill him. The camera turns to reveal he is talking to Sam about the incident, and he continues by saying he has not harassed Sam because he considers him a "good guy" — a "hou yahn." When Wong says he wished he had killed the young gangster, since he subsequently saw him out of jail enjoying life with Kwun, Sam counters that Wong must also be a "good guy," since he did not kill the kid even though he shot him six times. When Wong tries to get Sam to turn against his boss, Sam refuses and remains loyal to the Ngai family. They seem to share a common notion of "decency" — of what it means to be a "good guy" — in their compassion for the young and loyalty to their superiors. However, each misjudges the other. Wong orders a hit on Ngai Kwun through Mary, and Sam, to save his life, must go against the Ngai family — unwittingly in league with the police against the triads and undermining his own code of underworld chivalry.

Lau and Chan use the same words to describe their desire to be "righteous" or "virtuous." They both want to be "good guys."

Chan and Lau ask others for their opinion of their moral status — from Dr. Lee and Mary to Superintendents Luk and Wong. However, while Chan constantly verbally reiterates his identity as a cop, linking it with his moral status as a "good guy," Lau focuses on his identity as "good" or "bad," rather than cop or triad. Professional identity takes a back seat to morality, just as Confucius's "superior man" (or "gentleman") need not be a noble by blood and his "small man" need not be inferior by birth.

In *Infernal Affairs I*, similar gestures act as bookends for the narrative. Chan's first meeting with Wong on the roof coincides with the funeral of his other mentor Superintendent Yip. Chan, unable to come out from undercover to attend the funeral, salutes the hearse while hidden in the shadows. At the end of the film, Lau, a hero, salutes Chan's grave. Cleared with Dr. Lee's help, Chan has been posthumously recognized as a cop. Ironically, the funeral allows Lau to further solidify his identity as a hero who killed Billy, the mole who supposedly assassinated Chan, and the triad kingpin Sam. The more murderous Lau gets, the closer he seems to come to being recognized as "virtuous" by the state.

In fact, both Lau and Chan testify to the decay of the moral order through their inability to adhere to even the most basic Confucian precepts. Estranged from his biological father, Chan infiltrates his family, using his blood connection, in order to destroy his half-brother, Ngai. Even after he discovers his police mentor Wong conspired to have his biological father assassinated, Chan still believes in the just operation of the state, and he prepares documents to insure Ngai will go to prison. Ngai has trusted his half-brother, brought him into the illicit family business, and literally invited him into the family portrait by insisting he appear in a group photo taken to celebrate Ngai's daughter's birthday (Still 3.4). Ngai discovers Chan's police wire as he dies in his half-brother's arms, but Chan continues to work for the police force that killed his kin.

Still 3.4 *Infernal Affairs II:* Ngai family portrait

Although not wanting to work for a family embroiled in illegal activities that had likely treated Chan and his mother coolly (at best) is understandable, the passion with which Chan pursues his quest to eradicate crime borders on mania. In *Infernal Affairs II*, for example, the cellmate, whom Chan had beaten and sent to the infirmary, returns. That night he begins to sob in the cell. Chan asks if he still suffers from the beating, but the inmate dissolves into tears on Chan's shoulder because he was not granted permission to go to his father's funeral. Chan, of course, did not shed a tear when his father Kwun died; and, in fact, repeatedly asked for every opportunity to bring the Ngai family to justice. To convince Wong to allow him to go undercover, he says be wants to be "righteous." However, others have their suspicions — including Superintendent Luk. For Ngai, for example, it is inconceivable that Chan would choose the law and the state above his own family.[4] This jail scene contrasts Chan with a common criminal, and Chan, who has no filial sentiment, is found wanting.

Similarly, Chan's treatment of Keung — from the moment they first meet and Chan binds him to a chain link fence to beat him to the time when Chan falsely exposes Keung as a police spy posthumously — falls far below the Confucian ideal. Keung often reminds Chan that they are "brothers" in the triads, and Keung makes every effort (although a common criminal) to treat Chan accordingly. When Sam turns against Chan, Keung argues for his life — trying to hang on to the only other triad member lower in rank than he. Keung also lies to protect his triad brother when Chan goes against Sam's orders and leaves the others in order to get a "massage," but actually to meet Wong. After the meeting turns deadly, Keung rescues Chan from both the police and the other gangsters, who have converged to capture the mole. Fatally wounded, Keung says he hopes the masseuse was not ugly or else his death would somehow not be worthwhile. Keung dies in Chan's arms. Ever opportunistic, Chan uses Keung's death to take suspicion away from him by leaking Keung's name to the press as the mole. Although Chan may be a cop and a "good guy," he violates the laws of filial piety by refusing his obligations to his paternal family as well as the trust that should exist between sworn brothers. As such, he comes off worse than the criminals he tries to imprison.

If Chan goes against Confucian principles because of his commitment to vengeance against a corrupt father or because of his idealistic belief in the justice of the state, Lau defies this order for very different reasons. Lau's blood relatives do not appear in *Infernal Affairs*. Rather, in *Infernal Affairs II*, Lau tells Sam's wife Mary that he decided not to follow his family when they emigrated from Hong Kong. The implication seems to be that Lau's desire for Mary has kept him in Hong Kong and taken him away from his filial duty to his natal family. From there, Lau betrays each of his mentors on both sides of the law; e.g., arranging for Mary's death, assassinating Sam and Billy, and orchestrating the circumstances that lead to Wong's death. After Mary's death, personal desire continues to drive Lau with the new Mary in his life and the promise of a comfortable home and secure salary outweighing any moral sense of an obligation to either the triads or the police.

If Confucianism rests on the primacy of hierarchical interpersonal relationships, Lau positions himself quite differently. While being questioned during a review for promotion within the police force, Lau, speaking in English, expresses his views about his position after 1997: "Chinese people are sentimental. I hope the law will continue to back me up. But, I strongly believe in myself, sir!" Certainly, Lau's strong belief in his own desire puts him very much at odds with the sentiments associated with Chinese traditional philosophies like Confucianism.

Within the Confucian patriarchal tradition, sons ensure the continuation of the family name, the maintenance of rituals associated with honoring the ancestors, etc. Lau and Chan each have a daughter. All of their close police and triad associates — Sam, Wong, Keung, Yeung, Luk, as well as the entire Ngai family — have been killed. Lau's paralysis and Chan's death mark the end of the line. Allegorically, this can be read in one of two ways; i.e., that traditional Confucian values have exhausted themselves or, the opposite, that the world must change in order to come back into line with Confucian thought. In other words, the representatives of the state must be righteous so that criminals can be brought to justice without the moral quagmire opened up by the infiltration of moles on either side of the law; or, from the opposite point of view, Confucian values lead to corruption and affiliations based on filial piety, blood ties, and patriarchal rights must be eliminated.

Here, *Infernal Affairs* differs from more traditional morality stories. Although the corruption of the films' characters appears to be crystal clear, the path to "righteousness" or being a "good guy" remains murky. Unlike traditional morality tales, *Infernal Affairs* has no discernable moral center. Rather, all the principals may, indeed, end up in Avici hell, and, in a corrupt world, "righteousness" has little meaning. Unlike traditional allegories, too, *Infernal Affairs* holds out the opposite possibility — that traditional morality breeds corruption and that those disenfranchised from it (e.g., women, Communists) represent hope for the future.

Although the winks and smiles that become part of the replaying of Chan's expulsion from the academy and Dr. Lee's faith in his righteousness seem to beg a reading of *Infernal Affairs* that can recoup Chan as a "good guy," the trilogy's last sequence returns to the moral quagmire. On his cell phone with Wong, Chan walks down the street toward the stereo store. He explains why he had to shoot Shen in the leg, and he tells Wong he should learn to "write reports" like Yeung. Given that Yeung had demonstrated his desire to advance his career by breaking the law and writing "reports" to cover his tracks, Chan seems to valorize Yeung's methods — which parallel Wong's (although Wong had gotten caught). Chan goes into the store to make his drug drop before Lau enters to make a stereo purchase, and the cycle repeats itself. Chan, who tries to do the right thing by bringing Lau to justice, does eventually succeed, and the corrupt Wong and Yeung do, indeed, die. However, the films do not seem as sure about whether the "ends justified the means," and the final title leaves open the question of whether Chan and Lau really are the "people of the like" who find themselves doomed to the same level of hell.

With its depiction of internal hearings and various types of litigation, *Infernal Affairs* may also bear some resemblance to the vision of hell, Feng Du, held by China's third major religion Daoism (Taoism). In this hell, judges determine suitable punishments for earthly crimes within an elaborate spectral administrative system. The "Hell money" that Uncle John, a member of the Ngai family, burns to help the ghosts of the assassinated bribe their way up the ladder in the underworld mirrors the corruption of the earthly order. Just as Internal Affairs judges ruled not to prosecute Wong for murder or even demote him, the judges in Feng Du may be able to be persuaded to turn a blind eye to some offenses in the afterlife. Again, the certainty of any religious allegory cautioning against bad behavior goes up in smoke (Still 3.5).

Still 3.5   *Infernal Affairs II:* hell money

Post-Colonial Allegory: Hong Kong and 1997

Thus, the moral allegory exhausts itself, and the possibility of looking at *Infernal Affairs* as a political allegory about the Chinese nation and the transformation of the colonial state emerges. In fact, this switch in approach actually rests on overlapping concerns between national identity and religion. After the handover, this controversy has been brought into the open by the operation of the Falun Gong in Hong Kong. Illegal in the PRC, the Falun Gong operates legally in Hong Kong. Based on Buddhist doctrines and exercises involving *qi gong* (the cultivation of internal energy), the Falun Gong has been labeled an "evil cult" by some and recognized as a legitimate Buddhist sect by others. Although the reference may be oblique, the Avici Hell does have "unlimited space" reserved for those who persecute Buddhists and desecrate their religious shrines. With its crackdown on Falun Gong public demonstrations against PRC policies, the SAR police and courts may fall into this category.

Fredric Jameson has remarked that all third world literature narrates an allegory of the nation.[5] While controversy surrounds this assertion as well as whether Hong Kong should be considered "third world" or a "nation" in any sense of the term, many Hong Kong films can be approached as allegories of post-colonialism. Many scholars have looked at Hong Kong films leading up to the 1997 change of sovereignty as allegories about Hong Kong in relation to the concept of the Chinese nation.[6] Stephen Teo has termed this the "China syndrome" and Esther Yau calls it "1997 consciousness."[7] If anything, after 1997, allusions to the relationship between Hong Kong and the PRC in the cinema have become even more pronounced. However, the "imagined community,"[8] to which Hong Kong belongs, slips in and out of sight within these allegorical configurations.

Many allegorical associations appear to be quite obvious in *Infernal Affairs*. For example, the handover inaugurates a fifty-year period of "one country, two systems." In the trilogy, there is one society operating under "two systems" — the official world of the police (the government) and the "unofficial" world of the triads (business). Both moles Lau and Chan represent single individuals with dual identities — one for each "system" in which they must operate. Hong Kong, similarly, must operate under two systems simultaneously — one associated with the PRC, Communist party political rule, Chinese nationalism, and a post-socialist market economy; the other associated with British colonialism, a rigid bureaucracy and powerful civil service, a complicated welfare system, and a deceptively "free" capitalist economy with complex transnational connections.[9]

Infernal Affairs approaches the question of the nation differently at different points in the trilogy.[10] At times, the nation represents state powers — primarily, Britain and the PRC. Hong Kong exists within a post-colonial frame — somewhere between the United Kingdom and the PRC. At other times, the nation functions more as a repository of ethnic Chinese culture and traditions that transcend political borders. However, the trilogy also chronicles a sense of Hong Kong's unique identity as an SAR — constantly negotiating its separateness from the PRC, while avoiding any overt schism. Thus, the Chinese "nation" is not always tantamount to the "nation-state" of either the PRC or the ROC, but constantly in flux as a concept involving local identity, national sovereignty, and transnational links within Greater China and the rest of the world.[11]

Character relationships in *Infernal Affairs* map out a geopolitics of Hong Kong's sense of identity. The police department stands in for the government at large — colonial and British before 1997, post-colonial and transitional after the establishment of Hong Kong as an SAR of the PRC. The triads represent the commercial private sector — capitalism in its raw form with deadly competition over markets and products with a transnational reach. The institutions of mass media/popular culture and psychiatry mediate these two worlds and act as a chorus in the film commenting on and making sense of the struggle between the state and capitalism. The state must be seen to "police" the marketplace — keeping the excesses of capitalism in check, assuring "fair trade," protecting the "consumer" from "dangerous" commodities like cocaine and heroin. It protects the local — Hong Kong as a body politic under threat — from the dangers of the global — international drug trafficking.[12] As a snapshot of a specific time (1991–2003), the *Infernal Affairs* trilogy charts the relationship between the government and the economy before and after 1997 through its allegory involving cops and crooks.

Infernal Affairs II depicts the moment of the change of sovereignty on July 1, 1997, in relation to the lives of its central characters. *Infernal Affairs III* continues by mapping out the changes in these relationships as a result of the handover with a close look at the relationship between the PRC (i.e., Mainland police) and local Hong Kong criminal affairs. *Infernal Affairs I*, however, provides a more subtle rendering of the impact of 1997. No direct mention is made of either July 1, 1997, or of any connection between the Hong Kong and PRC governments. However, allegory lives on insinuations and subtleties, and *Infernal Affairs I* does not paint a bright picture of post-1997 Hong Kong.

In *Infernal Affairs I*, pre-1997 appears only as a framing memory of the British colonial police academy and the streets of Hong Kong dominated by petty criminals. Although the corruption of the police force has been initiated, Sam's moles do not have the strength to move in any major way within the force until after 1997. As the film opens, the police force mourns the death of Superintendent Yip, a holdover from the British colonial administration. Superintendent Wong, another officer from the colonial regime, has difficulty maintaining control. His undercover operative Chan may be having a mental breakdown, a major drug sting goes wrong, and he must deal with the realization that Sam has a mole in his operation. He can no longer trust his subordinates, and his map of the borders separating criminals from the police must be readjusted. Casting Eurasian actor Anthony Wong in this role helps to underscore the point that European authority can no longer be taken for granted. Wong's death later in the film marks the absolute end of an era of British governance.

However, the representatives of capitalism (albeit, its "dark" side) are also suffering from a post-1997 malaise. The triad's plan to solidify its contacts in Southeast Asia, specifically Thailand, fails to materialize. On July 2, 1997, the day after Hong Kong's sovereignty changed, Thailand devalued its currency, the Thai baht, in relation to the US dollar. Most economists point to this as the start of the crisis that had been brewing, and the rest of Asia (with some key exceptions like the PRC) fell like dominoes.

In *Infernal Affairs*, Thailand becomes the source of economic woes that put the profitability of the triads in doubt. Frustrated, Sam (standing in for Hong Kong business) looks at the government (the infiltration of an undercover cop) as the ultimate cause of the economic crisis at hand. Unable to contain his anger, Sam, likely suspecting Chan hides a police wire in the plaster cast around his broken arm, grabs Chan's cast and smashes it on a table. Chan writhes in agony, but no wires appear. Sam, like the Hong Kong capitalists, cannot seem to articulate what went wrong. He lashes out, but he makes no progress in rectifying the situation.

The fact that Sam has all his triad underlings fill out employment forms in order to try to determine the identity of the mole makes this turn of events comic. Lau plans to use the forms to check the triads against computerized police records. The gangsters laugh that Sam plans to enroll them in the Mandatory Provident Fund (MPF) — a social security service provided by the state for its "official" labor force. Working in the unofficial, illegal economy, the triads still fall prey to a bureaucracy that does not serve their needs. Again, the state's commitment to leveling the excesses of capitalism by providing for the basic welfare of its citizens becomes an issue. Ironically, the difficulty one of the gang has in filling out this form leads to Chan's discovery of Lau as Sam's mole — the plot to unearth the mole with bureaucratic paperwork backfires.

Sam's and Wong's deaths mark the passing of the old order in both colonial administration and in international business practices. Both represent traditions that inevitably will be replaced. Lau's participation in Chan's funeral near *Infernal Affairs I*'s conclusion highlights this, as well as the corruption and impotence of the younger generation of bureaucrats (police) and businessmen (triads). Lau has emerged at the top in each field; i.e., he replaces Sam as drug kingpin and Wong as head of the Internal Affairs investigation into the infiltration of the police. However, as a triad mole who wants to remain an "honest" cop, he stands as a mockery of both systems. He epitomizes a crisis in government and business with no solution in sight. Dying without exposing the mole, Chan also symbolizes that crisis. Although posthumously cleared and buried with honors as a police hero, Chan's death does not restore any sense of confidence in the just running of the state. Rather, the pomp and circumstance of the funeral presided over by Lau mocks the very notion of justice.

The tip of the red PRC flag flutters at the border of a shot of the blue sky of Hong Kong. Moving back from the grave featuring Chan's photo, flowers, and an inscription praising his contribution of his body and the perpetuation of his "spirit," the camera eventually shows the bagpipes and drums associated with a formal British colonial burial. In full dress uniform, Lau steps up to salute the grave (Still 3.6). Others follow his lead to honor Chan in the presence of Dr. Lee, May, and the daughter he never knew he fathered. Chan represents failure — as a cop unable to bring the crook to justice, as a father unable to provide for his family, and as a lover who did not fulfill his promise to return to his beloved. With the Communist flag and the colonial ceremony, presumably, he has also failed as both a former British and current Chinese subject.

Still 3.6   *Infernal Affairs:* Lau salutes at grave

Lau's salute takes on mythic proportions; the fluttering flag, dress uniform, rigid salute, pipes and drums all conjure up a mythic empire. In "Myth Today," Roland Barthes discusses a strikingly similar image:

> I am at the barber's, and a copy of *Paris-Match* is offered to me. On the cover, a young Negro in a French uniform is saluting, with his eyes uplifted, probably fixed on a fold of the tricolour. All this is the *meaning* of the picture. But, whether naively or not, I see very well what it signifies to me: that France is a great Empire, that all her sons, without any colour discrimination, faithfully serve under her flag, and that there is no better answer to the detractors of an alleged colonialism than the zeal shown by this Negro in serving his so-called oppressors.[13]

Lau's salute references the authority and legitimacy of two distinct nations — Britain and China. Shutting his eyes to savor the moment, Lau seems to slide effortlessly into both the old colonial order and the current SAR under the sovereignty of the PRC flag. The surface of the image testifies to the smooth transition. A picture of colonial success the officer only adds to the strength of the nation; the change of sovereignty has not diminished his zeal to serve the state. However, Lau, the chameleon representing Hong Kong, lives a lie. The surface of the myth — as Barthes argues — naturalizes and reifies a lie. Lau/Hong Kong may desire to be a loyal colonial and/or Chinese subject, and may, indeed, even live under the impression that he is one; however, the truth of the matter — disavowed by the spectacle and Lau's warped psychology — is that this gesture of submission to the authority of the state is a sham.

Although an alternate ending for PRC release and the eventual working out of the plot in *Infernal Affairs III* seem to right this situation, this version of *Infernal Affairs I* ends without containing the crisis. Although 2003 clearly saw more massive crises (e.g., SARS, the mass demonstrations on July 1 around the controversial "Article 23" anti-subversion law, etc.), 2002, the year in which *Infernal Affairs I* was both produced and set, did not see Hong Kong smoothly sailing along in a sea of political, economic, and social bliss. Rather, Hong Kong's chief executive, Tung Chee-hwa, a businessman rather than a politician, who came to office after Chris Patten, the last British colonial governor of Hong Kong left, continued to lose popular support. In 2002, Tung, unopposed, began his second term in office without holding a popular election.[14] Although SARS and "Article 23" did not help his situation in 2003, Tung's popularly steadily declined from 1997 to 2002. (In fact, Tung finally stepped down in 2005.)[15]

With a police bureaucracy divided against itself (e.g., Internal Affairs, Organized Crime and Triad Bureau, Central Investigation

Bureau) and vying for control over daily operations and a business world of triads, bitterly divided but relentlessly moving toward a monopolistic economy (cartels) that exacerbates the vicissitudes of capitalism, *Infernal Affairs* mirrors the crisis in the authority of the state, economic decline, and social unrest, which characterized Hong Kong at the time the film was produced. Although *Infernal Affairs I* does not directly mention 1997, the implications seem clear. Positioned, like Lau, with one eye on the Chinese flag and one ear attuned to the British imperial pipes and drums, Tung Chee-hwa stands precariously between the commercial sector he comes from and the public government he leads.

Given that political conditions in China historically have worked against direct expression of dissent, China, as Jerome Silbergeld points out, has a long tradition of allegory in the literary and visual arts: "Allegory, ... by any name, is a well-conditioned cultural response that no politically sensitive Chinese artist, visual or textual, modern or traditional in period, has needed to think too much about in order to use."[16] Constrained by colonial censorship, commercial Hong Kong films rarely dealt directly with topics of geopolitical significance since the British censorship regulations expressly forbade any material that might agitate its neighboring countries. That Hong Kong cinema should continue in this vein does not come as much of a surprise.

In fact, the very direct treatments of the political conditions leading up to 1997 and the consequences of the increasingly visible role of the PRC within Hong Kong after 1997 in *Infernal Affairs II* and *Infernal Affairs III* stand out. Although tamed by the melodramatic frame of the gangster family saga in *Infernal Affairs II* and Lau's eventual comeuppance in *Infernal Affairs III*, the fact that both films so obviously deal with Hong Kong/PRC political relations contrasts sharply with *Infernal Affairs I*'s more biting, but less obvious post-colonial (and, perhaps, post-national)[17] allegory.

The trilogy begins, and *Infernal Affairs II* takes up, the story in 1991. Up to 1991, the colonial governor appointed all the members of the Legislative Council, and 1991 was the first year that limited elections were held for this body under Governor David Wilson. The last governor of Hong Kong, Chris Patten, a conservative politician on a mission to bring some semblance of democracy to the colony before the end of British rule, took office in July 1992. Many questioned his mission as a last ditch effort on the part of the British colonials to "prove" their democratic and enlightened superiority to the totalitarian Chinese. Resonating with the "infernal" path depicted in the trilogy, one PRC representative once called Patten an "eternal sinner"/"sinner of a thousand generations".[18] However, his popular electoral reforms continue to operate — often causing friction with Beijing over the voting franchise — into the 21st century.

Infernal Affairs II chronicles the last year of David Wilson's term of office and the Patten years. Providing the back-story for the lives of Lau and Chan in 2002, this film looks closely at the impact of the handover on the lives of cops and crooks. In both camps, it narrates a changing of the guard as the lives of the film's characters metamorphose in relation to Hong Kong's transformation from a British colony into an SAR of the PRC. Emigration out of the colony increased during this period, and people, like Lau in *Infernal Affairs II*, were asked to account for their reasons for staying in Hong Kong. However, the exodus from Hong Kong had another dimension, as many carried multiple travel documents and shuttled back and forth between Hong Kong and North America, Europe, Australia, New Zealand, etc. When Ngai plans to hand over his business affairs and emigrate, Sam, rightly, suspects it is a ruse to solidify his power in Hong Kong. Moreover, emigration for the Ngai clan proved to be literally a dead end, since the entire family met a bloody fate in Hawaii.[19] In fact, the Ngai family resembles failed attempts by actual triad members to reestablish themselves abroad.[20] The American paradise did not supply a safe haven for the Hong Kong businessman, and others who left Hong Kong before 1997 also began to see greater opportunities in Asia and return.

Food and Family: Triad Connections and the Passing of the Old Order

As the opening scene of *Infernal Affairs II* shows, the traditional operations of cop and crook revolve around an elaborate system of "guan xi" — in which personal relations are used to curry favor and maneuver advantageously within the ethnic Chinese world.[21] As Mayfair Yang indicates with the title of her book, "gifts, favors, and banquets" form the material dimension of these connections. In the first scene of the film, Wong makes an attempt to curry favor with Sam by providing a "banquet" of Styrofoam containers filled with carry-out food. Although Sam eats lustily, the rather pitiful attempt fails, and Sam refuses to turn on his triad boss. The scene echoes the one in *Infernal Affairs I* in which the *guan xi* bond between Sam and Wong is ripped apart by the realization that each plans to betray the other through their moles. Sam, who has been eating his "banquet" of Styrofoam carry-out dishes, uses his arm to sweep the food to the floor to indicate his anger at Wong's infiltration of his gang. Times have changed and old *guan xi* relationships no longer prove viable.

In fact, *guan xi* networks operate in *Infernal Affairs II* through food — established restaurants, sidewalk "cafes" (*dai pai dong*), and celebratory family meals. Eating is a very serious matter, and relationships formed around food and drink structure the hierarchical worlds of both the criminals and the police. At one point in the film, in a rare private moment with Sam who has police protection while waiting for Ngai's trial, Lau serves his boss tea and calls him "big brother." The ritual of serving tea to a superior to reinforce a hierarchical bond runs deep within the *guan xi* culture, and Lau and Sam easily slide into their roles as triad superior and underling.

Early in *Infernal Affairs II*, two meals in which the future for the cops and the crooks comes under discussion are juxtaposed. Cadet Chan (before his expulsion), Head of the Police Academy Yip, and Superintendent Luk sit down for a formal meal and discuss the implications of 1997 for the police force. Yip, who sees himself as part of the older generation associated with colonial rule, plans to train the younger generation (specifically, Chan) for the new order. Based on Confucian precepts, the template for *guan xi* relationships comes from the traditional model for patriarchal family obligations with filial piety at the heart of those relationships. While a guest at his table, Yip publicly makes a commitment to Chan as his protégé with Luk as his witness. However, the question of loyalty becomes complicated by the personal nature of the *guan xi* relationship, and the vicissitudes of Chan's obligations to his mentors, as well as to the Hong Kong government under the British and then under the SAR/PRC, subtend the plot. (Indeed, the primacy of blood within *guan xi* relations complicates the matter in the following scene in which Chan Wing-yan's half-brother Ngai Wing-hau — the same character "wing" ["yong"] which means "forever," used as the first part of the given name of each, marks them as part of the same generation of boys within the Ngai family — appears to announce their father's death and set in motion the series of events that lead to Chan's expulsion from the academy and life undercover.)

In the next sequence, four gangsters within the Ngai family orbit — the "Big Four" of Negro, Ching, Wah, and Gandhi — meet at a hotpot restaurant to discuss their future after the murder of Kwun (Still 3.7). The bubbling pot of broth in the center of the round table alludes to the fact that their plot could easily boil over, burning them, and that their business affairs and destinies are intertwined since they eat out of the same bowl. Ngai's death has heated things up, and, sweating around the hotpot, the four decide not to continue to pay the Ngai family a share from their triad enterprises. With the patriarch Kwun dead, the son does not merit the same respect. Just as Ngai's after-dinner presence turned his brother Chan's stomach in the previous sequence, Sam appears at the hot pot place, grabbing a chair from one table and a bowl and chopsticks from another, to help himself to the food. Negro, Ching, Wah, and Gandhi do not want to talk business with this close associate of Ngai, but Sam, smiling, assures them he is just there to eat. In fact, Sam only needs to eat and pass the phone around so that Ngai can threaten two of the gang with taking advantage of a third (cuckolding him and stealing his drugs) and the other two fall in line to maintain the status quo with the new head of the Ngai family in charge. Ngai skillfully uses *guan xi* in order to get them to do his bidding. The system works, and Ngai maintains the triad hierarchy he inherited from his father.

Still 3.7 *Infernal Affairs II:* hot pot

   Meanwhile, the police, headed by Luk and Wong, remain outside eating ice cream from a convenience store — away from the heat of the hotpot — expecting a gang war in the wake of Ngai's murder. Disappointed and frustrated by the smooth transition, they go to meet Ngai at a *dai pai dong*, which was his late father's favorite after-hours haunt. A *dai pai dong* can be anything from a vendor with a basket of snacks to an outdoor eating establishment with a "kitchen" and several tables. Although originally licensed, the "big poster" licenses are no longer issued. Newer, unlicensed establishments — usually outdoor and temporary — now operate "unofficially." With their own marginal status, these "moveable feasts" attract a loyal following for the quality of the food or for the inability of the proprietor or clientele to go easily to the police to report any misbehavior. Ngai goes to this *dai pai dong,* because his father had started his triad career there in the illegal gambling business — the bottom rung of the criminal ladder. Wearing wire-rim glasses, plain button down shirts, cardigan sweaters, and simply tailored suits throughout most of the film, Ngai does not seem to fit into the less prosperous and less formal world of the *dai pai dong.* However, the juxtaposition of the well-to-do, urbane, well-educated, younger generation with the immigrant, impoverished, uneducated older generation of Hong Kong inhabitants allows the space to contain the old and the new Hong Kong simultaneously. For Ngai, the *dai pai dong* offers a fitting place to mourn the passing of his father (and the old Hong Kong) as well as a location from which he can solidify his own power as heir to that past.

Wong, supported by Luk, harasses Ngai, but, before things can get out of hand, Sam arrives to stand between the police and Ngai's gang in order to defuse the situation. Again, Sam's *guan xi,* associated with food, enables him to act as mediator — in this case, between the triads and the law, rather than between two competing triad groups. Sam reminds Wong to respect mourning (i.e., Ngai's filial obligations to his father), and Wong backs down. Later, Sam's disruption of the ritual food offerings in Thailand when he moves to kill Ngai's assassins places him unwittingly in the same camp as Wong, who orchestrated Kwun's murder. Like Wong, his violent disregard of ritual pushes him out of the network he counted on for his livelihood. With rituals surrounding food out of whack, Sam falls victim to a bullet in a café in the Thai depot and his wife Mary nearly falls victim to rape when Lau brings her a bag of groceries in her hideout in the New Territories in Hong Kong.

In the *dai pai dong*, Ngai's act of mourning for his father takes on a more profound significance, since it establishes his legitimate authority within the gang based on Confucian tradition. Honoring the dead, Ngai takes a cigarette, lights it, takes a puff, and places it upright in an untouched bowl of rice as an offering to the spirit of his father (Still 3.8). Continuing the ritual, Ngai leads the gang in a toast to his father by pouring a libation on the ground for his spirit and using two hands to down a drink in his honor with one gulp. The gang does likewise, and, as the piano swells on the soundtrack, the tableau of the gang, in silhouette, mourning the loss of its old leader and tacitly agreeing to the new marks a traditional passing of power within the triads. (Later, this gesture of mourning reverberates with Chan's lack of affect as he comforts his filial fellow inmate who cries when he cannot attend the memorial for his father's death.)

Still 3.8 *Infernal Affairs II:* cigarette offering

Torn by his commitment to what he sees as a just state rather than a corrupt family in which patriarchal relations based on blood never worked in his favor, Chan tries to negotiate his way within the *guan xi* network of the Ngai family. His first major failure involves his inability to establish himself as head of a family, and he destroys a restaurant kitchen when his girlfriend announces she has had an abortion because she does not want her child growing up in the triads. In fact, throughout the trilogy, triad business, intermingled with personal affairs (really, the very essence of *guan xi*), takes place in bars and restaurants. The "Big Four" have their "office" in the hot pot restaurant, Ngai does business at the *dai pai dong*, and Sam runs what looks like a bar/restaurant with a more upscale atmosphere presided over by an oversized painting of the Three Graces. Whereas Sam seems at ease eating at any of these establishments, Chan never appears to fit in — tearing up kitchens, staying on the sidelines at his niece's birthday party, and attacking other gangsters at posh Western restaurants. Outside the traditional networks, Chan's police wire reveals his lack of "connection" to Ngai when his brother sees it as he dies at the *dai pai dong*.

Infernal Affairs' eateries, in fact, serve as locations for violence — often ritualized gangster assassinations. Two of the "Big Four" are killed in or near restaurants — one set on fire with the hot pot, and the other shot by an assassin who had been admiring fish in a restaurant tank while waiting for his mark to be sent to "sleep with the fishes." At the *dai pai dong*, Ngai orders his underling Law to execute three of his gang involved with Kwun's murder. Ngai then takes the gun and kills Law, whom he has uncovered as a police mole. Uncle John, the Ngai family enforcer, builds up the fire in the street shrine near the *dai pai dong*, and he begins to burn spirit money for the dead as the bodies are put in the flames. Again, food and rituals surrounding death combine — spirit money (a.k.a. Hell banknotes) give the ghosts they have created an easier time in the afterlife and bribe them to go quickly on their way away from the world of the living. *Guan xi* operates in hell as it does on earth.

One of the major turning points in *Infernal Affairs II* occurs at the Jumbo Floating Restaurant in Aberdeen (Still 3.9). Up to this point, Ngai appears to be, like Sam, a "real triad" — traditional, committed to the gangs, contemptuous of government authority. His earlier decision to leave the triads and pass his business along to the "Big Four" and Sam had simply been a ploy to orchestrate their deaths and solidify his narcotics operation in Thailand. However, now, in 1997, Ngai voices what appears to be a sincere wish to bring the family "out of the shadows" by campaigning for political office within what will become the SAR. At Jumbo, Ngai attends a reception for some of the new mainland Chinese functionaries who oversee the handover. Lavishly decorated with murals in traditional Chinese design and a formal, Chinese-style staircase, the Jumbo restaurant provides an ideal backdrop for the meeting of Hong Kong business and PRC bureaucracy. A major tourist attraction, Jumbo does not enjoy much popularity among Hong Kong locals, but it has become a favorite of mainland tourists eager to sample Hong Kong cuisine in a massive and sumptuously outfitted establishment. As its English name "Jumbo" implies, the restaurant, ablaze at night with electric lights, can be overwhelming — very much like the influx of PRC functionaries in Hong Kong from the massive nation across the border.

Still 3.9 *Infernal Affairs II:* Jumbo restaurant

In a pinstriped suit with a flower on his lapel, the bespectacled Ngai fits in well with the other Hong Kong businessmen trying to establish *guan xi* with the new regime. When the family's triad connections come up, Ngai's lawyer quickly steps in to smooth things over by saying that his client has been acting as an informant. However, Ngai's political ambitions come to an abrupt halt when Superintendent Wong, accompanied by an entourage of police officers, arrives to arrest him. The series of events leading to Ngai's death before July 1, 1997, and his downfall as a gangster begin at Jumbo and end at the *dai pai dong*. The police gun down Ngai, who has been manipulated into pulling a gun on Sam, at the *dai pai dong* — marking the end of Ngai and his entire family (with the exception of the snitch Chan).

Warshow has called the gangster "tragic," and the full force of this tragedy can be felt in this scene. Like Lau, Ngai strives to disassociate himself from the triads, but he cannot escape his fate. The fact this happens at a *dai pai dong* — associated with Ngai's father's as well as Hong Kong's past — gives the scene an allegorical dimension. The triad ritual and folk traditions associated with Ngai die with him — the world of the local, unlicensed, "unofficial" economy of Hong Kong under colonial rule ends at the *dai pai dong*.

As depicted in *Infernal Affairs II*, the handover at midnight June 30–July 1, 1997, combines mourning for the loss of loved ones (and, implicitly, Hong Kong) with a sense of nostalgia for colonial (and, implicitly, triad) ritual into a celebration of transformation. For Wong, the Ngai family has been eliminated, but a new threat, in the form of Sam, emerges. As the fireworks burst in celebration, Sam, looking at a photo of his deceased wife, Mary, sheds a tear for her (and, implicitly, Hong Kong) before he joins in the celebration in the next room (Still 3.10). The celebrants have little PRC flags, and Sam toasts the new Hong Kong with a full glass of brandy (Still 3.11) — echoing the gesture of mourning

Still 3.10   *Infernal Affairs II:* Sam's photo with Mary

Still 3.11   *Infernal Affairs II:* Sam joins party

and celebration of the new triad boss at the *dai pai dong* in honor of Ngai Kwun's death and Ngai Wing-hau's ascent to power. Time seems cyclical. Since the "future" of all the characters has already been established in *Infernal Affairs I*, this sequence takes on a quality of foreboding as well. It points to a complex set of possibilities associated with the change in sovereignty that have economic, political, social, and personal consequences for the characters in the film as symbols of Hong Kong.

"The Rule of Law": Policing Hong Kong

Given *Infernal Affairs* tells a story about law and order, it does not seem odd it includes scenes devoted to litigation — hearings that involve the state's methods of determining guilt and innocence by defining crimes and their punishments. Before and after the handover, discussions of Hong Kong's Basic Law and the principle of the "rule of law" became very common elements of the public discourse.[22] Questions arose regarding the relationship between the written law and various agencies of the state able to determine the meaning of the law and execute its operation. In other words, concerns were voiced — and continue to be expressed — in Hong Kong about the relative independence of the judiciary from political or other influences coming across the border. This "rule of law" has important ramifications for business, since it assures contracts and other business matters are subject to clearly defined regulations.

However, the "rule of law" does not always favor traditional methods of handling grievances or commercial transactions. For example, in his study of Hong Kong's political elite, Bob Beatty quotes an official as saying:

> We shouldn't let the "traditional Chinese side" of our culture begin
> to creep into us. Because there are people who say that the laws

here is Western law and isn't suited to Chinese culture ... We definitely disagree with those people who say that the law is based on Western culture. It's not. It represents the values which most people believe in — a clean, uncorrupted system, a just criminal system, fair to everybody — these are the things we believe in, believe that we need, and believe that we should defend in Hong Kong.[23]

Although a "rational," "democratic" society should be based on the "rule of law" rather than the fancy of individuals with power or the whim of a particular political faction, the law does not always satisfy the desire for justice, and frustration with the law finds expression in popular culture. As mentioned above, *Infernal Affairs II* operates on the premise that SP Wong, frustrated with the lack of justice of a system that gave his partner's killer a new lease on life, takes matters into his own hands and conspires with Mary to kill Kwun. Connections/*guan xi* fill the void left by the failure of the state.

Wong's hearings conjure up a history of litigation involving the Hong Kong police. Since the institution of the force in 1844, the Hong Kong police suffered from endemic corruption revolving around protection or "tea money" paid to officers to turn a blind eye to various illegal activities. The situation finally came to a head in 1973 when a probe targeted a respected officer, Peter Fitzroy Godber. (Rumors circulated that the police closed ranks and allowed Godber to escape in order to cover up his misdeeds.) As a consequence of this case, the Hong Kong colonial governor, Sir Murray MacLehose, made the decision to establish the Independent Commission Against Corruption (ICAC) in order to take cases of police corruption away from the Internal Affairs/Internal Anti-Corruption office.[24]

As mentioned above, a public relations campaign was mounted to promote the new commission, and several budding New Wave filmmakers (including Ann Hui) directed television films to promote its efficacy. Commercial features like *Anti-Corruption*

(1975) and *Jumping Ash* (1976) dealt with similar themes as well. In fact, police corruption continues to be an important theme within the triad genre (e.g., Kirk Wong's *Organized Crime and Triad Bureau*, 1994; Eric Tsang's *Tigers*, 1991, which features both Andy Lau and Tony Leung as cops on the take investigated by the ICAC). In Lawrence Ah Mon's *Lee Rock* series (1991–2), Andy Lau plays the titular protagonist based on a Hong Kong police officer, corrupted by the triads and pursued by the ICAC, who found safe haven in Taiwan.

However, the ICAC remains outside the scope of *Infernal Affairs'* narrative. Rather, in *Infernal Affairs*, corruption becomes an internal matter and subject to issues of justice rather than graft and greed. In fact, money only comes up as an issue at one point in *Infernal Affairs III* when Wong notices Chan's hefty savings account. However, the charges that the police closed ranks to protect Godber find a parallel in Wong's hearings. For the "greater good," the rule of law is set aside, and Wong is cleared to resume his duties.

Although Shen, representing the occult powers of mainland China with its own difficulties in governing through the "rule of law," comes in to save the day in *Infernal Affairs III*, the courts never come into play in establishing a just and uncorrupt police force at the conclusion of the trilogy. The mole Lau self-destructs before he can be tried and found guilty — internal commissions as well as the ICAC seem pointless. Rather, each instance of the operation of judicial procedure in *Infernal Affairs* turns the "rule of law" into a farce. Not only do the police manipulate others into committing crimes (e.g., Wong, Yeung), use their own information as triad members to eliminate the competition (e.g., Lau), and allow gangsters to make a mockery of police procedure (e.g., Ngai), but the working of the internal system to maintain an uncorrupted police force both unwittingly and knowingly subverts the "rule of law" in each instance in which it is evoked in the trilogy.

The internal police hearing in which Wong is exonerated for the murder of Kwun in *Infernal Affairs II* parallels the hearing in which Lau's killing of Billy is deemed justified in *Infernal Affairs III*. While the police department makes a conscious decision to cover-up an admitted criminal act by one of its officers in the first case, the second case exemplifies the state's ability to be easily duped by a crafty criminal. Both instances testify to a crisis in the operation of the state through the criminal justice system in which the rule of law is subverted. In both cases, the outcome of the hearings is a *fait accompli* in the narrative. Since Wong's hearing takes place before the events in *Infernal Affairs I*, it is clear that he is exonerated. Similarly, the deliberation of the panel in the hearing involving Lau takes place off-screen while Lau freely walks about outside under a bright blue sky on-screen. The process lacks gravity in the narrative, since the outcome has been predetermined within the workings of the plot.

In the case of Wong, court action is far from swift. The eleventh internal hearing takes place in 1997, based on a tape recorded and in police possession since 1995, in which Wong talks about his conspiracy to murder Kwun in 1991. Faced with the very visible evidence of the tape, Wong admitted his culpability in 1995. However, immediately before his death, SP Luk indicated the police force would not condemn Wong for his actions. Rather, the force would rally behind him in order to continue to press their case against Ngai. Faced by a panel of three judges in a shadowy room filled with scattered files, Wong again admits he committed a crime. As Luk predicted, the judges offer a way for him to start over.

This scene is intercut with Lau's interview in English for promotion within the force. Lau is very much like Wong. Neither has much faith in judicial process. On the rooftop in the climactic scene of *Infernal Affairs I*, Lau begs Chan for a second chance to prove himself a righteous member of the force. Chan continues the arrest procedure, opting to leave Lau's fate to the courts. When

Lau's triad brother Billy steps in and kills Chan, Lau does not follow through with Chan's plan to bring Lau's triad associations out in the open. Rather, in *Infernal Affairs III*, he plots to eliminate the other moles before he can be detected. Just as Wong turned to murder in his frustration with the criminal justice system, Lau opts out and also decides to recreate himself as a righteous cop through murder.

Although Wong admits that he has "no confidence left" and that he "lost," the panel, supported by a portrait of Queen Elizabeth II on the wall behind them, gives Wong an Interpol file and another chance to defeat Ngai. The judge remarks that "the Ngai family does not run Hong Kong," and brings the "incident" to an official close. The shadowy, backroom deliberation of the police internal hearing places the government on a par with Ngai's underground operations. The Interpol file points to a transnational police system beyond Hong Kong, and the portrait of the Queen insists on an imperial sense of justice in which the colonial administration refuses to be bested by locals (Still 3.12). Lau's self-confident assertion that he will do well after the handover in his newly elevated rank is also sworn under a portrait of the Queen (Still 3.13). Since Wong's

Still 3.12 *Infernal Affairs II:* Wong (back to camera) with portrait of the Queen

Still 3.13 *Infernal Affairs II:* Lau with portrait of the Queen

hearing reaffirms the relative nature of justice and criminality within the colony, Lau makes a good point. A triad mole, indeed, may do well under either regime.

Lau's internal hearing in *Infernal Affairs III* also fails to bring the "truth" to light. However, in this case, the system appears not to collude with the criminal to cover up a murder, but, rather, to be ignorant of the actual nature of the crime. Lau had, in *Infernal Affairs II*, won his promotion through his convincing identification with the police administration. In *Infernal Affairs III*, what started as performance begins to take on the trappings of delusion as Lau appears to believe in the version of events he narrates for the judges. Again, as in Wong's hearing and Lau's promotion, the process creates the persona the individual takes on as "righteous" cop rather than heinous criminal.

Unlike Wong, Lau meets his judges in a bright conference room. The voice of the adjudicator continues as images of documents support Lau's story beginning with his "heroic" killing of Sam. A black and white iteration of events on the roof with Chan and Billy indicates that Lau's casting of himself as police hero has become the official version of the story, and the Central Investigation Bureau (CIB) deems Billy's killing "legal." Although inconvenienced by a stint in Administration, Lau happily returns to his duties in Internal Affairs after a month. The system has operated in his favor at the service of injustice. The "rule of law" becomes moot, since no internal or independent court hearing ever brings a criminal to justice in the trilogy. Only an insistent feeling of a crisis in the legitimacy of the state remains. However, although a character representing the PRC does step in to fill that vacuum of state authority, his actions remain outside the "rule of law." The PRC government has no authority to police the HKSAR, and any covert action on the part of the Mainland government — no matter how well intended or "righteous" — remains clearly outside the "rule of law" and the "one country, two systems" agreement.

National Shadows: Mainland Connections

Infernal Affairs III introduces the first major character in the trilogy from the PRC, Shen/Shadow, and makes the relationship between Hong Kong and mainland China a central concern of the plot. In addition, just as Lau represents Internal Affairs, another new character Superintendent Yeung embodies "external affairs," as part of the Security Wing that oversees Hong Kong/overseas police concerns involving SAR security; e.g., terrorist threats, etc. At a time when questions of sedition were part of a public discourse involving the controversial Article 23 that would broadly define acts of treason and government powers to handle incidents of actual and suspected subversion, Yeung appears as the embodiment of fears about the powers of the state to control the loyalties of its citizenry. Yeung's own loyalties and methods remain suspect throughout most of the film, and this echoes the feelings of many of the people who turned out in massive demonstrations against Article 23. William Overholt defines the controversy as follows:

> ... in July 2003, the Hong Kong government proposed to pass stringent Article 23 legislation with elements that attracted widespread opposition. In particular, the law would have allowed an Assistant Police Commissioner (rather than the courts) to authorize searches of private homes, allowed the government to proscribe organizations proscribed on the Mainland (Falun Gong and the Roman Catholic Church are proscribed there), allowed the Secretary for Security rather than the courts to set the rules for appealing such decisions, and precluded a public interest defense against a conviction for publishing state secrets. (On the Mainland, almost anything can be a state secret.)[25]

The demonstrations on July 1, 2003, led the government to back down, and the PRC appeased the public by stepping up its economic reforms that would allow Hong Kong enterprise easier access in

China as well as other pecuniary boons. However, the political ups and downs continued throughout the year in which *Infernal Affairs III* was in production and, eventually, had its premiere.

Played by Beijing-born Leon Lai, Yeung represents a point of mediation between the PRC and Hong Kong, and, not surprisingly, he develops a close bond with Shen in order to bring Lau's true identity as a triad to light. Without Shen, Yeung does not seem to be up to the task, and Yeung needs his Chinese connections to flush out Lau. The allegorical significance of the Hong Kong government needing the help of a PRC official in order to set things right in the SAR develops as a consequence of the unfolding of the plot. Given that Shen survives as the only principal police character to live to the end of the trilogy also appears to point in the direction of reading *Infernal Affairs* as a story about the inevitability of the erasure of the border between the PRC and the SAR. Hong Kong needs China in 2003, and it will be China in less than fifty years.

In this regard, *Infernal Affairs III* positions itself in opposition to another popular Hong Kong film on triads, the police, and gangsters from across the border, Johnny Mak's *The Long Arm of the Law* (1984). Referencing the actual activities of the Big Circle Gang from the PRC, this film links criminal activity with Chinese Communism out of control as Hong Kong suffers from a crime wave headed by a former Red Guard from the Great Proletarian Cultural Revolution (1966–76). In Michael Mak's *Long Arm of the Law III* (1989), Andy Lau plays Li Cheung-kong, a former member of the People's Liberation Army who ends up as part of the Big Circle Gang in Hong Kong on the lam from Mainland officials. Undercover as a former member of the PRC government with ties to the army, Shen resembles the former Red Guard and the former PLA soldier from the *Long Arm of the Law* series as well as the officials sent to Hong Kong to deal with the border-crossing gangsters. In fact, Shen turns out to be *Infernal Affairs III*'s main hero, emerging from China as Hong Kong's savior.

Infernal Affairs III, as opposed to *The Long Arm of the Law* in which the Royal Hong Kong Police appear as corrupt and brutal, also rehabilitates the Hong Kong police through Yeung. The devious cop who tortures his criminal charges becomes the pillar of honesty when he ferrets out the mole Lau with the help of his PRC counterpart. *Infernal Affairs III* obliterates any ambivalence about the functioning of the remnants of the colonial state in league with the representatives of the Chinese nation felt in *The Long Arm of the Law*. As Shen moves off into an uncertain future in the film, he joins other PRC officers who have come and gone on Hong Kong screens since the 1980s, including Do Do Cheng in *Her Fatal Ways* series (1991–94) and Jet Li as *The Bodyguard From Beijing* (1994).

Of course, *Infernal Affairs III*'s treatment of Hong Kong/PRC connections extends beyond the operation of the police as representative of the government into the world of commerce. Even in *Infernal Affairs II*, triad business operations take the PRC market more seriously. When Police Cadet Chan captures Keung in the act of stealing a car, the gangster claims he has an order in from a Mainland client for a Mercedes. In *Infernal Affairs III*, on the phone during one of his sessions with Dr. Lee, Chan talks about several deals involving cars going across the border to cities like Zhuhai. In fact, within all sectors of the economy, 2003 marked an increased visibility of Hong Kong's economic reliance on the PRC.

Moving between 2002 and 2003, *Infernal Affairs III* skims over the political crises and economic changes involving Hong Kong's relationship with the PRC, while alluding indirectly to dramatic changes that have taken place between the time of Chan's funeral and the time of Lau's confinement to a wheelchair. For example, *Infernal Affairs III* does not directly mention the SARS epidemic (March 13–June 22, 2003); however, a significant part of the plot revolves around issues of pathology (albeit psychopathology) set in doctors' offices, hospital corridors, and, finally, a sanitarium. Lau's interactions with ghosts in both the hospital waiting room and the sanitarium parallel the eeriness of those locations associated with media reports on the epidemic ravaging hospitals, quarantining many health care institutions, and creating casualties.

SARS also exacerbated the existing tensions between Beijing and the HKSAR, since the disease likely originated in the wild game markets of neighboring Guangdong Province, and many blamed the PRC for trying to cover up the severity of the disease as it ravaged China. However, the PRC quickly came to the aid of Hong Kong business — one of the main sectors from which it counts on political support. Although it may be ironic that the same people (or their children) who fled the PRC after its establishment in 1949 now support it as a friend of "free enterprise," Beijing has many staunch supporters from the business sector who have made enormous profits from investment across the border and the increased commercial activity within Hong Kong as a result. As SARS cut deeply into all sectors of the Hong Kong economy, PRC initiatives to ease travel of Mainlanders into Hong Kong helped to pick up some of the slump in tourism when the medical crisis finally abated. In addition, although it did not fully take effect until January 1, 2004, Hong Kong and the PRC signed the Closer Economic Partnership Agreement (CEPA) in June 2003. Ahead of the implementation of the WTO agreements, CEPA gives Hong Kong privileged access to a wide range of PRC business opportunities, services, and goods. Politically, tensions calmed when the controversial Article 23 anti-subversion bill was put on the back burner, and *Infernal Affairs III* projects a picture of Hong Kong and the PRC working closely together to combat crime.

In fact, Yeung, savvy and ambitious, first appears in the film in a scene in which he attempts to get ahead in the police department by exposing Taiwanese gangsters in order to ingratiate himself with his PRC counterparts. In order to nab two weapons dealers from the ROC, Yeung threatens some petty Hong Kong gangsters, plants drugs on them, and coaxes them into attacking the Taiwanese. When the uniformed police arrive, he tells them to use the drugs as an excuse for beating up on the two older arms dealers. Later in the film, Yeung gets his reward for the set-up. Since the Taiwanese have no objection, a police delegation from the PRC plans to pick up the arms dealers. Yeung and his staff discuss, in detail, a "shopping and eating" expedition for the Mainlanders, with a side trip to Macau to make certain they see all the sights. Clearly, Yeung sees his own standing enhanced by using the Taiwanese to elevate himself in the eyes of Beijing.

Also, the introduction of the illegal arms market marks a change in direction for the trilogy. Previously, the illegal economy revolved around illicit narcotics.[26] The shift from heroin to cocaine in *Infernal Affairs II* signaled a triad decision to move into a potentially wider and more lucrative market. Also, this change marked a move away from the local economy in which several small dealers imported drugs from South America into a larger, monopolistic enterprise in which a single triad kingpin controlled the bulk of the product through a Thai middleman. In *Infernal Affairs III*, a further shift occurs when Shen's group approaches Sam to go into the arms business. In this case, the business becomes inextricably tied to national politics. The PRC arms dealers move in on the ROC gangsters' turf, and their ability to make this move results from Shen's ties to the People's Liberation Army and implicit corruption within the Chinese military.

Sam, a "real triad," seems suspicious of his new business partners from the beginning. Again, the Taiwan connection becomes salient. Hong Kong triads have a long and deep connection with the KMT. In 1947, during the civil war against the Communists, KMT Lieutenant General Kot Siu-Wong amalgamated the triads into the 14K Society (referring to the address of its headquarters coupled with a "K" for gold/money) in order to help with the fight against Mao and his forces. (Of course, Chiang Kai-Shek's involvement with the triads goes back even further, and the underworld was deeply involved with the bloody purge of the Communists from the KMT in 1927 as well as with the looting of China as Chiang set up his capital in Taipei in 1949.) After 1949, anti-Communist triads as well as legitimate KMT supporters ended up in Hong Kong, having no future in the PRC.[27] The film biography *Lord of the East China Sea* (1993), for example, chronicles the life of Du Yue-Sheng, a key link between the KMT and the triads in Shanghai, who ended up in Hong Kong after 1949. The bloody riots occasioned by a dispute over the display of the ROC flag during the October 10 (Double Ten, Nationalist Day) celebrations in 1956 testified to the enormous strength of both the KMT and the KMT-connected triads in Hong Kong.[28] In fact, the 1956 riots led to the establishment of the Triad Society Bureau within the Criminal Investigation Department (CID), which later became the Organized Crime and Triad Bureau (OCTB).[29]

Although illegal arms have a long tradition within triad circles, these Northerners from Shanxi do not fit in with Sam's notion of an operation that had been the domain of triads based in Taiwan. After putting his least competent underling in charge of Mainland affairs, Sam plots to set up Chan, whom he suspects of disloyalty, by using him to test Shen. Sam orders Chan to attack Liang, Shen's brother, expecting Shen to murder Chan. However, after hitting Chan over the head with a liquor bottle, Shen calls them even and begins to plan a transaction with Sam. However, Sam, confiding in and also warning Chan, asks him why Shen decided not to kill him. Convinced his suspicions about Shen have some merit, Sam asks Chan to take charge of the PRC arms transaction. Of course, Sam has met with Yeung to set Shen up for a bust, and Sam has withheld the arms so that the Mainland gangsters would kill Chan. However, when Chan shoots Shen in the leg and Shen wounds Chan in the arm, both realize that neither is a gangster. When Yeung arrives on the scene, Shen holds a gun to Chan's head. Yeung encourages him to kill Chan and save him the trouble of arresting him, but Shen reveals his own and Chan's true identities when he says that Chan is not Sam's man. All lower their guns and the three officers of the law — from Hong Kong and the PRC — discover they are, indeed, on the same side, and Shen asks his Hong Kong counterparts to speak Mandarin so he can understand them better. Later, Shen's bullet finally brings down Lau and restores a semblance of order to the Hong Kong police by eliminating the last of Sam's moles.

However, looking at *Infernal Affairs* as an allegory about the legitimate right of the PRC to step out of the "shadows" to participate more fully in Hong Kong affairs for the greater good of the citizenry on both sides of the border may really miss the point. The mercurial nature of the identities of Yeung and Shen makes the ultimate revelation that both are "good guys" ring a bit false. In fact, the solidity of national identity appears to be just as slippery as their moral identities. Shen, for example, plans to quit his life as an undercover operative after the botched arms sting, and Yeung continues to operate on the outer edges of professional ethics as he frames underworld figures, manipulates triads into helping him advance his career, and drives one of Sam's moles to suicide in his presence. In fact, the flawed characters and malleable identities of all the "good guys" in the trilogy put the concept of a solid national identity and a belief in a just state in doubt. Hong Kong moves from the colonial administration with a transnational economy into a post-colonial order with a transitional government overseen by a rapidly changing Communist state with a post-socialist economy. The "master narrative"[30] of liberation from imperialism breaks down, and it is not replaced with any clearly defined preference for the "good old days" of British colonialism. This vertiginous state of affairs puts any clear "national" allegory in doubt and pushes the trilogy (and Hong Kong) into the post-national as part of the postmodern condition of late capitalism.

4

Postmodern Allegory:
The Global Economy and New Technologies

All of the signifiers of modernity only go one way — down — in *Infernal Affairs*. The elevator, riddled with bullet holes, which boxes in Lau with Chan's and Billy's corpses embodies the hellish trap of modern life that can only descend. SP Wong falls from the heights of a modern office building only to land crushed on a taxi — the promise of upward mobility dashed in one image that also drags down the legitimacy of state power. All the indicators of modern "progress" point in a downward direction. Liberation from colonialism, the promise of modern technology, and the potential pleasures of global consumer capitalism fall from the heights as well.

Postmodern texts tend to favor allegory. Fredric Jameson, among many others, has commented on the parallels between the slippery signifiers of allegory in which the sign always stands in for something else and the uncertainty and contingency that characterize postmodernism. As Jameson notes, this newer type of allegory demands a process of interpretation that is:

... a kind of scanning that, moving back and forth across the text, readjusts its terms in constant modification of a type quite different from our stereotypes of some static medieval or biblical decoding, and which one would be tempted (were it not also an old-fashioned word!) to characterize as dialectical.[1]

In fact, *Infernal Affairs* slips among allegorical associations with religion, morality, nation, as well as with a more general condition of postmodern life. The certainties of time, space, and identity have evaporated. Like many postmodern texts that allegorize speed, compression of time, and reconfiguration of the past as part of the present moment, *Infernal Affairs* has an obsessive interest in time and dates as well as a pervasive atmosphere of nostalgia, mourning, loss and abandonment. This interest in time can be interpreted as allegorizing Hong Kong's change in sovereignty or as an exploration of the processes of globalization under late capitalism.[2] Esther C. M. Yau notes the way in which the local and global crises parallel one another within Hong Kong's film culture:

... Hong Kong movies are as much about this world city's paradoxes in a politically unusual and compressed time (that is, the 1997 handover) as they are about a technical culture's race for global economic opportunities and cultural capital. These movies equally anticipate and register the impact of a high-speed race for profit against the barriers of time and distance.[3]

James A. Steintrager makes a similar point:

It appears that the combination of uniqueness — there is no other situation quite like Hong Kong's at this time — and generalizability — are not capitalism and technology pushing all of us in a similar direction? — has produced a cinema that has a purchase on critical spectators everywhere.[4]

As Jameson notes, within postmodern culture, allegory moves far beyond the national:

> On the global scale, allegory allows the most random, minute, or isolated landscapes to function as a figurative machinery in which questions about the system and its control over the local ceaselessly rise and fall, with a fluidity that has no equivalent in those older national allegories ...[5]

Like many films about drug trafficking, *Infernal Affairs* chronicles changes in patterns of consumption, the production of commodities, leisure and labor within late capitalism. The drug becomes a special commodity — and favorite screen fetish.[6] In the postmodern turn, the commodity can be stripped of its substance and become an image, which, in turn, becomes a commodity. The cinematic fantasies surrounding drugs mirror a seldom articulated anxiety surrounding the production, circulation, and consumption of commodities more generally.

Like coffee, tea, tobacco, sugar, rum, silk, cotton, and the other key products that built colonial empires, drugs generally come from impoverished former colonies — countries still ravaged by neo-colonial and dependent economies. They are processed, repackaged, and re-exported through entrepôts like the port city of Hong Kong, and they make their way back to the former colonial centers for consumption. Instead of providing a happy picture of "economic development," however, the drug trade symbolizes the fear of transnational trade, the exploitation of labor as those involved in the trafficking risk their lives and the lives of others for profit, and the ill effects of the commodity on the consumer whose body becomes consumed through addiction.

The cinematic depiction contains enormous contradictions. The source of the drugs plays on xenophobic fears of poverty, ignorance, and envy on the part of the producers of the raw materials.

However, it also highlights the ill effects of transnational capitalism — bypassing the laws of the state in order to maximize profits by looking for the cheapest and most desperate laborers on the planet. The underworld traffickers appear on screen as hated gangsters, ruthless competitors who will kill to corner the market and make more money. However, this picture also describes the successful "legitimate" businessman who can cunningly circumnavigate the globe for the most advantageous deals and aggressively attack the competition. The drug addict, too, may not be that far removed from the contemporary consumer — addicted to shopping, riddled with debt, hounded by credit card companies rather than loan sharks.

In fact, films about the drug trade provide a rare opportunity for filmgoers to indulge in fantasies about the ills of consumer capitalism. However, in most of these films, any critique of capitalist exploitation remains safely in check by the depiction of the operation of the state. A slew of cinematic police officers, detectives, lawyers, judges, social workers, psychiatrists, corrections officers, and other public servants leap into action to keep the underground narcotics economy under control. However, as the nation-state loses its grip on the economy, countries take a backseat to the needs of transnational corporate interests. The erosion of manufacturing jobs, the diminution of salaries with a shift from skilled labor to service sector employment, the push to an information based economy that leaves the undereducated majority behind as a permanent underclass, the rise of global cartels that lessen market competition, privatization of key government services, the decay of social welfare policies, and the general impoverishment of the working classes describe a broad range of contemporary post-Fordist economies from Europe and the United States to Japan and Hong Kong.

Infernal Affairs chronicles these economic changes through drugs. Given that Hong Kong likely would not exist if it were not for the Opium Wars and the international drug trade as it developed in the 19th century, the territory has a particularly close historical connection to drugs as commodities. Up to the early part of the 20th century, the Hong Kong government received a significant share of its revenue from taxing the opium trade. Several of the buildings in Hong Kong celebrate its roots in opium. The distinctive circular windows of Jardine House, visible in one scene in the trilogy, meant to resemble the portholes on ships that made Jardine-Matheson one of the wealthiest opium trade concerns during the early rise of Hong Kong as a port, loom over the drug deals and police stings of the 21st century.

The Ngai family's fortunes parallel the changes in the drug economy as well as the larger Hong Kong economy during the post-1949 period. As Mao put an end to opium smoking in the PRC, the business modernized across the border — moving from opium (smoked) to heroin (injected), from a population of addicted coolies and fallen landowners to a younger generation of junkies and prostitutes, many of whom were refugees down on their luck. After 1949, exile capital from China flooded Hong Kong along with the refugees who also provided cheap labor. Ngai Kwun clearly got his start catering to this population with the hope of winning it big in the numbers game.

His son, however, inherits new economic circumstances. Cheap labor now stays across the Chinese border. Hong Kong continues to operate as a middleman — a center of trade, banking, tourism, information, and a service-oriented economy — but the small factories that built the postwar economy have disappeared. The subculture of addicted junkies becomes less profitable than the patronage of the middle classes, and cocaine replaces heroin as the drug of choice for the upwardly mobile. Rather than needing to be anesthetized against the pain of prostitution or other forms of alienating and physically debilitating labor, the better educated, more affluent drug users need a boost to stay on top of their money-making potential. Cocaine gives an edge to white collar workers up all night to get ahead in the stock market, real estate speculation, or the design/information sector. It adds to the speed and intensity of lavish parties put on to impress clients and keep them on their feet for business meetings the next day. Ngai Wing-hau understands the change in the market and swiftly moves to strengthen his investments in cocaine.

In fact, Ngai models this new consumer. Unlike his father who prefers to relax at the *dai pai dong* or play traditional Chinese music at the Hong Kong Chinese Martial Arts Association, Ngai, in glasses, cardigan sweaters, and business suits, with a house filled with books, rich wood furniture, and overstuffed chairs that could easily come from a bourgeois British or American home, cuts a figure that is not at all out of keeping with the contemporary transnational businessman. In fact, both cops and crooks take this as the standard of middle-class, cosmopolitan living. Although Sam wears colorful polyester print shirts to do his business in the streets, his inner sanctum at his bar/restaurant sets a very different tone with wood paneling, neo-classical European painting, Buddhist objects d'art, and a general "tastefulness" in line with a global bourgeois standard. Sam's wife Mary also has a tastefully decorated office/living quarters in her warehouse with Venetian blinds, fresh flowers, and a high priced stereo. Within the postmodern amalgamation of styles, a framed print of a Red Guard from the Cultural Revolution, drained of its political significance, becomes another element of the elegant interior decor.

Dr. Lee's wood paneled office featuring a relaxing English landscape painting fits in with this general sense of a middle-class norm defined by interior design within *Infernal Affairs'* mise-en-scène. This reaches its apogee with Lau and his bride Mary's newly furnished apartment. Entranced with commodities like Rolex watches and expensive sound systems, Lau and Mary take inordinate care with the decoration of their new apartment —

discussing the placement of the sofa, size of the ottoman, and the precise organization of the design elements of the flat.

Golf also becomes a way of defining this bourgeois lifestyle on both sides of the law. In *Infernal Affairs I*, Lau learns about his promotion when he is invited up to a golf practice session on the roof with his police superiors. At the reception at Jumbo restaurant in *Infernal Affairs II*, Hong Kong and PRC bureaucrats compare notes on golf courses, and Ngai tries to relax by practicing his putting at his home. Cops and crooks prefer similar cars, similar suits, and similar lifestyles.

Again, Lau and Chan serve as emblems of two sides of the new economy. Both have the flexible identities necessary to move quickly between various competing spheres. They operate within the same system of consumer capitalism that enables them to bond while enjoying the sale/purchase of electronic goods. At first, Chan may not seem to fit in with the veneer of bourgeois respectability associated with Ngai, Lau, and both Marys. After leaving the cushy life at the police academy, Chan becomes a very scruffy gangster — perpetually wearing a few days' growth of beard and a leather jacket. His swollen bank account, too, seems to indicate he has no interest in financial investments of any kind. Even though he appreciates stereo equipment and a quality snort of cocaine, he does not appear to have any home or any clear display of conspicuous consumption. Constantly on the phone and on the move, Chan travels light moving between the worlds of cop and crook — dealing in information and the circulation of commodities like stolen cars and cocaine. Lau also deals in information and the circulation of drugs. However, he enjoys the benefits of the new economy more than Chan. An upwardly mobile public servant with a credit card, Lau can afford and expect as his right the bourgeois lifestyle promised by consumer capitalism. Winners and losers in the new economy, both Lau and Chan trade on their flexibility, adaptability, and knowledge of communication, information, and new technologies, as well as their violence and ruthless drive to get ahead.

Ngai's enterprise also embodies another commercial trend. As he makes his operation more efficient within the dynamics of the global marketplace, he solidifies his power in a cartel. Eventually, he corners the market by literally killing off the competition. As global concerns become more powerful, less dependent on the laws of any given nation-state, and more flexible in their ability to move production facilities, labor, capital, and goods around the world, they grow and drive out the competition. Sam, of course, benefits from this consolidation, and he banks on the weakening of the state occasioned by the 1997 handover. Constantly trying to position himself between the triads (Ngai) and the state (SP Wong), Sam, like many transnational businessmen who play off older, more established, and less flexible international businesses against the rigidity of the state (e.g., taxes, tariffs, trade regulations, etc.), Sam profits from the rivalry between Ngai and Wong. Even though his heart may be with the traditional triads, he enters a new world in 1997 because of his ability to manipulate both the business world and the state for his own benefit.

Ending *Infernal Affairs I* with Lau in uniform at Chan's grave makes a very compelling statement about the government's susceptibility to internal corruption because of capitalism run amok. Several scenes in the trilogy revolve around internal reviews and judicial actions, and they depict a popular culture version of how the government functions behind closed doors. The first taste of the occult workings of the state comes at the beginning of the trilogy with Chan's expulsion from the academy and recruitment as an undercover officer. At first, it seems difficult to tell whether the secrecy surrounding Chan involves the fear of leaks to the triads or competition among various police agencies for access to information. In fact, the line between corruption and ambition within the police force happens to be very thin. Wong and Luk work as much against as with each other in *Infernal Affairs II* as they each operate a different mole within the Ngai organization. In *Infernal Affairs III*, the fact that the ambitious and conniving Yeung, who "bends" the law to arrest the Taiwanese, is not a villain comes as a surprise when his relationship to the undercover agent Shen comes out in the open. Throughout the film, he works against Internal Affairs as much as with it — keeping Lau's colleagues ignorant of his suspicions until the bloody climax. The cloak and dagger operations of the Security Wing involved in state security makes Yeung's character even more suspect as an agent with uncertain allegiances.

Suspicion runs deep in the trilogy — an indication of a general feeling that the government may not be using its authority for the public good. *Infernal Affairs II*, as noted above, begins with Wong's expression of dissatisfaction with police procedure. However, Wong's motivation remains muddled. The hit may be Wong's only way to achieve a sense of justice in an unjust world, it could be to settle a score and get even with a gang that took advantage of his leniency, or it could be an expression of his personal ambition to get ahead in the police force by eliminating a triad kingpin and putting a more amiable leader Sam in his place. If predisposed to see the police as "good guys," Wong can be justified in his actions as upholding the "spirit" of the law by eliminating a gangster. If a more cynical view of the state as an oppressive force holds sway, then Wong becomes a cold-blooded killer who abuses his authority for his own ambitions.

This scene, like many others in *Infernal Affairs II*, alludes to *The Godfather* (1972). Francis Ford Coppola's film opens with a man, Bonasera (Salvatore Corsitto) petitioning Don Corleone (Marlon Brando) for justice. When Bonasera's daughter is severely beaten, the American criminal justice system does little to rectify the wrong done to the family, so he turns to the mafia for justice. An Italian émigré Bonasera worked hard in America, believing in the American dream, but he had that dream crushed with the assault on his daughter that did not lead to the type of criminal penalty he expected. The conversation takes place in shadows — in Corleone's private office. Similarly, the opening scene of *Infernal Affairs II* begins in shadows with Wong speaking to an unidentified off-screen figure about the circumstances of his first arrest and murder of his partner (Still 4.1).

Still 4.1   *Infernal Affairs II:* Wong in opening sequence

In this case, the reverse shot reveals that Wong petitions Sam for justice — trying to convince him to turn on his boss Ngai so that Wong can avenge his partner's death. Just as Bonasera turns to the mafia for justice, Wong turns to the triads. However, while Bonasera is an undertaker with less of a commitment to the American nation-state, Wong, as a cop turning to the triads, marks a more severe lack of confidence in the authority of the state. As the scene in *Infernal Affairs II* resonates with the opening of *The Godfather*, however, something else comes into play in the postmodern allegory. The crisis extends beyond questions of the legitimacy of the nation-state into the realm of spectacles about the state. The chiaroscuro lighting, use of close shots, nearly direct address to the camera, and the shock of the reverse shot to show the addressee in the scene comments as much on intertextuality and the international history of motion picture narratives as it does on the specific workings of the criminal justice system in any given nation. The allegory becomes slippery — moving outside of the national allegory and into the transnational.

Information from Hell: New Technologies

Infernal Affairs envisions the movement of the global economy from processed raw materials driving imperialism (e.g., opium) to manufactured goods (e.g., electronics like stereos) at the base of postwar neocolonialism to the postmodern "information society" in which communication becomes commodified, and the economy moves from a base in production (of material things) to one based on reproduction (replication of images and information). Although cars, electronics, and drugs still circulate, Lau and Chan, as moles, primarily deal in information. Their labor obtains its value from their ability to inform on the secret plans of the opposing camp. "Forgotten Times" played on stereo equipment with outmoded vacuum tubes prominently on display contrasts with the trilogy's use of new technologies as the conduit for Lau's and Chan's circulation of information. In many ways, *Infernal Affairs* provides a portrait of the new economy through its depiction of new technologies in action in the marketplace of information.

When the undercover cop and his handler meet up on the roof for the first time in *Infernal Affairs*, Wong gives Chan a tracking device and a watch — references to technological mastery of space and time. Chan jokes about sticking his wire into his body to make his job as snitch even more efficient and permanent. The next scene featuring Lau and technology seems to put Chan, who cannot tell the difference between a watch and a hidden camera, at a clear disadvantage. Surrounded by maps and a bank of computer monitors, Lau easily takes command of space and time within the digital environment. The mise-en-scène emphasizes Lau's surveillance of the wider space of the city as well as the map of the suspect's worried face, as he sits in a holding area sweating out his wait for the interrogation to begin. A master of deception and in command of multiple identities, Lau easily tricks the gangster into divulging the location of his illicit transaction by using a cell phone to contact his brother, thus enabling Lau to triangulate on the location of the warehouse using satellite technology. Electronic mastery of time and space linked to Lau's "flexible" persona delivers results.

A general environment of paranoia envelops both the camps of the cops and the crooks during the Thai drug deal. Cinematography emphasizes the blurred edge between surveillance and clandestine operations as it cuts between footage resembling washed out surveillance video and the contrasting textures of celluloid. The cops watch from a distance — Lau behind at a computer terminal — and the triads speculate on who may or may not be a cop as they remain alert as lookouts on the street. While Sam monitors the police channel, Wong switches the band used for transmission. As Wong tries to triangulate on the location of the deal using cell phones and satellite positioning, Sam replaces the cell phones to throw the cops off the scent and sends a car out as a decoy for the police to shadow.

Although Chan proved his powers of observation when he was recruited to work undercover by identifying Wong's mismatched socks, it is Lau's powers of observation that lead him to notice Wong's finger tapping linked to changes in strategy during the drug bust. As Wong calls off the tail on the decoy car and identifies the dock where the deal will take place, Lau monitors the tapping on his computer and discovers the Morse code communication. Using a text message on a cell phone, Lau alerts Sam to the bust and the drugs end up in the water before the police move in. As an observer with technical expertise and state of the art communication technology, Lau has outmaneuvered Chan. Tapping Morse code into his wire to communicate with Wong, Chan lags behind Lau's more sophisticated use of computers and cell phones to communicate with Sam.

As a commodity, cell phones are sold through marketing appeals to their ability to enhance communication.[7] Throughout

Infernal Affairs I, Lau's cell phone puts him on top, while the same technology undercuts Chan at every turn. The bad timing of a cell phone call alerts Lau to Chan's tail after the meeting with Sam at the cinema. Another cell phone call tells Chan that Sam has found the mole, since Lau has put a tail on Wong in order to catch him with his contact. Although Chan manages to escape, Wong is caught when the ruse of talking to his "wife" on his cell phone does not save him from being spotted by the triads sent in to nab him with his mole.

After Wong's death, Lau easily makes contact with Chan the mole using Wong's cell phone. After a few taps of Morse code, Chan happily makes contact with his new police handler Lau. Lau dupes Chan into setting a trap for Sam. Chan's tapping has led Lau to Sam, who is shocked that the ring of the cell phone call he places to his mole should be heard in the parking garage where he tries to escape from police capture (Still 4.2). Ironically, Sam has used the cell to call on his own executioner. Lau appears, cell phone in hand, and puts a bullet through Sam's head. In fact, throughout the trilogy, the cell phone replaces the pistol in the generic arsenal for both cops and crooks.

Still 4.2   *Infernal Affairs:* Sam with cell in parking garage

The computer also becomes a weapon in Lau's hands. Duped, Chan gives Lau the password for his confidential police computer file. Again, new technology turns against Chan as any hope of the recovery of his identity as an honest cop gets erased with the click of a computer mouse as the screen confirms "Empty Protected File." Chan becomes vulnerable because the computer file has, for all intents and purposes, become his identity. He relies on the digital archive to maintain his sense of self, and he has become a victim of what Jacques Derrida has described, in his ruminations on Freud and digital technologies via Nietzsche's polemic against the traditional historian and the archive, as "archive fever":

> There would indeed be no archive desire without the radical finitude, without the possibility of a forgetfulness which does not limit itself to repression. Above all, and this is the most serious, beyond or within this simple limit called finiteness or finitude, there is no archive fever without the threat of the death drive … There is not one archive fever, one limit or one suffering of memory among others: enlisting the in-finite, archive fever verges on radical evil.[8]

In *Infernal Affairs III*, even though Chan has been redeemed through the efforts of the psychiatrist Dr. Lee, Lau, verging on "radical evil," continues his relentless assault on the archive (from Dr. Lee's computer files to SP Yeung's cache of audiotapes) in a futile attempt to expunge the memory of his life as a triad mole. Of course, his archive fever, linked to the death drive, makes him suicidal, since he must effectively annihilate himself in order to achieve his goal.

Lau, certainly, has other difficulties with technology as well. Sam routinely records his clandestine conversations with Lau to hedge his bets in case his police mole decides to turn on him. (This parallels the routine recording of Wong's conversations by Sam's wife, Mary, in *Infernal Affairs II*.) However, the tape only emerges after Lau has killed Sam. While the tape damages his relationship with his wife Mary, it does not expose Lau as the mole, since another mole destroys it before it circulates to honest members of the police force. The tables have turned, however, and Lau continues to have technical trouble as the trilogy pits old against new technologies. A paper trail alerted Chan to Lau's identity as Sam's mole, and, eventually, Chan's identity is saved through paper archives as files from the late SP Yip finally surface.

Infernal Affairs II presents new technologies as "old." The gangsters carry oversized cell phones which were known, at the time, as "da ge da" (Mandarin) or "dai go dai" (Cantonese), literally, "big brother big," referring to the status given to the boss as "big brother" who needs a cell phone to operate his business. While the cops competitively bicker over notification of a possible bust on their cell phones, Sam and Ngai team up to use the "dai go dai" to convince Gandhi, Negro, and the others to back down from their bid to overturn Ngai as his father's successor. The use of the new cell phone technology underscores not only Ngai's power and ability, but his position as a "new" type of triad boss, able to change with the times. Ironically, in *Infernal Affairs II*, this makes Ngai look "old," since from the perspective of 2003, the technology from the early 1990s looks dated.

Later in *Infernal Affairs II*, the cell phone solidifies Ngai's power, saves Sam, and kills his wife Mary. While Ngai, in police custody, notes each ring of his cell phone as the death of an enemy, Mary manages to get through to Sam's cell in order to tell him that she ordered Kwun's death and Ngai plans to kill him. Also, Ngai has nailed SP Wong with the surveillance tape that uncovers Wong's conspiracy with Mary to kill Kwun, and technology appears, again, to be working in Ngai's favor. Using a land line to set up Mary, who has spurned his advances, Lau makes a final cell phone call to her before her death. Mary and Lau exchange glances at the airport and Mary recognizes Lau as the one placing the call, but she does not answer her cell, and a moment later Uncle John arrives to run her over and kill her.

Paralleling the two earlier scenes involving the exercise of Ngai's power through the cell phone, Sam and Ngai face off at the *dai pai dong* with cell phones rather than guns as their instruments of terror (Still 4.3). Cell phone calls confirm that Uncle John holds Sam's wife and infant child hostage in Thailand, while Sam's Thai associates have Ngai's entire family under the gun in Hawaii. Later, on the cell phone, Sam agrees to the murder of the Ngai family, and he takes possession of Ngai's role as master of new technology in the service of triad power. In *Infernal Affairs III*, Sam exercises power through technology in the scene in which he uses his cell phone to order Chan to attack Liang at the steakhouse — an exercise of muscle through remote control.

Still 4.3 *Infernal Affairs II:*
Russian roulette with cell phone

However, cell phones, tracking devices, digital cameras, CCTV (closed circuit television), and other types of surveillance technologies become more difficult to pin down in *Infernal Affairs III*. Technology, for example, begins to box Lau in. As the administrative inquiry into the deaths of Chan and Billy drag on because Billy (actually Lau) destroyed the CCTV camera in the elevator, Lau finds himself exiled to a desk with a telephone and computer monitor in an empty wing doing menial administrative tasks. Literally cut off from the rest of the force, Lau's only lines of communication are mediated through technology; i.e., the telephone and the computer screen. However, Lau, master of the menial, uses his administrative knowledge to spy on Yeung by manipulating the assignment of his designated parking space.

Lau returns to Internal Affairs and surrounds himself with neatly arranged pink files on his desk. Paper becomes a comforting echo of the past as well as a dead end path in the present. Like "Forgotten Times" played on the old stereo, archives of information stored on paper in file cabinets become part of the repressed substratum that structures the trilogy. In *Infernal Affairs II*, for example, Chan gives Wong the keys to an archive of files he has compiled to nail his half-brother Ngai. Papers compiled without the benefit of "spell check" software, Chan tells Wong to overlook the spelling errors in the documents. In *Infernal Affairs III*, Lau begins to follow a paper trail of still photographs trying to link Yeung, Shen, and Sam in order to determine whether or not Yeung could be one of Sam's moles who knows that Lau is indeed a triad "brother." A high-angle long shot shows Lau alone in a dusty archive dwarfed by stacks of file boxes (Still 4.4). Crouching on the floor, he laboriously goes through stacks of papers to uncover a photo of Shen with Sam.

Still 4.4   *Infernal Affairs III:* Lau in archive

For Lau, the archive — analogue and digital — mirrors the classic "trouble" Derrida sees as arising out of the slippery nature of the concept:

> Nothing is less reliable, nothing is less clear today than the word "archive" … Nothing is more troubled and more troubling. The trouble with what is troubling here is undoubtedly what troubles and muddles our vision (as they say in French), what inhibits sight and knowledge, but also the trouble of troubled and

troubling affairs (as they also say in French), the trouble of secrets, of plots of clandestineness, of half-private, half public conjurations, always at the unstable limit between public and private, between the family, the society, and the State, between the family and an intimacy even more private than the family, between oneself and oneself.[9]

Lau's hacking into Dr. Lee's computer archive puts his own sense of self in doubt as he imaginatively identifies with the deceased Chan through the mediation of cyberspace. The cyber-archive opens up their psychoanalytic and romantic relationship to Lau, and he immediately over-identifies with his nemesis. He troubles the borders between the public and the private, between the State (in the form of institutions of the criminal justice system as well as psychiatry) and the intimacy of heterosexual romance, as well as the boundaries that define his own identity. It also testifies to his contradictory desire to preserve and destroy the archive and (through identification with Chan) himself.

Lau also becomes obsessed with another archive, and he sets up an elaborate surveillance system in order to penetrate security at the Security Wing and uncover any information Yeung may have that could lead to Lau's exposure. However, as Lau identifies with the deceased Chan, he actually mirrors the living Yeung. Paranoid and crafty, Yeung and Lau think alike. When Lau plants a bug under Yeung's car, Yeung, suspicious, checks the surveillance device he has watching over his own vehicle. In fact, much of *Infernal Affairs III*'s narrative revolves around a battle of the "wire" as images from Yeung's computer surveillance vies with Lau's obsessive hours spying on Yeung in his insecure Security Wing office. With weakened eyes indicated by glasses, contact lenses, and eye drops, Yeung and Lau figure as computer nerds — completely wired, isolated in front of their monitors, hand on the mouse, trying to hack into some vaguely secret cyber-world just beyond their fingertips (Still 4.5).

Still 4.5 *Infernal Affairs:* Lau's eyes with mouse

Still 4.6 *Infernal Affairs III:* cyberspace

Lau cannot act without a wire, and all his actions are mediated through the computer. With his computer, he remotely monitors the water cooler in the Security Unit and begins his assault on Yeung's office via remote control by drugging the water supply (Still 4.6). He manages to get into Yeung's safe through his computer surveillance as well by drawing a bull's eye on a transparency over his monitor in order to decipher the combination. However, Yeung, the ultimate master of technology, is one step ahead of Lau, and, as Lau opens the safe, Yeung calls him on his cell phone to ask if he is having fun in the office. In addition to the surveillance on his car and office, Yeung, collaborating with Shen, had set up CCTV in Internal Affairs to monitor Lau. Caught in the act, Lau manages to elude Yeung, and, triumphant, parades his pilfered tapes in front of his staff at Internal Affairs. However, Lau's love affair with technology has soured, and, delusional, he ends up implicating himself as he plays the tapes in which he colludes with Sam. Still claiming to be a "hou yahn," Lau cannot grasp the fact his voice is featured on the tapes.

5

Identity as Static:
Surveillance, Psychoanalysis, and Performance

Within postmodernity, the integrity of the individual body fractures. The cell phone distances the body and the voice, and the voice becomes a ghostly echo from the past circulating through machinery like Tsai Chin's "Forgotten Times." In *Infernal Affairs III*, Lau becomes obsessed with controlling the voice; i.e., with finding and destroying the tapes of his conversations with Sam. In other words, he tries desperately to control an identity from which he has become totally alienated — and, of course, this endeavor proves futile. In his search for power over his own identity, he has lost any sense of the location of power within his environment. Technology has undone him. Communication and information media hopelessly confuse the operation of power and its impact on his sense of self. As Gilles Deleuze notes: "Occult power is confused with its effects, its supports, its media, its radios, its televisions, its microphones: it now only operates through the 'mechanical reproduction of images and of sounds.'"[1]

Watching, being aware of being watched, watching oneself, and the paranoia that comes from constant surveillance are all major visual, dramatic, and narrative themes in the *Infernal Affairs* trilogy. Characters like Lau look at themselves incessantly, living in terror of losing that image, paranoid of the consequences of losing the power to define identity. Moving from the mirror to the monitor, appearances on television mark the dissolution of personal identity. In *Infernal Affairs III*, Lau's glimpses of himself on closed circuit television mark his descent into madness (Still 5.1). As Jean Baudrillard states in "The Ecstasy of Communication": "With the television image — the television being the ultimate and perfect object for this new era — our own body and the whole surrounding universe become a control screen."[2]

Still 5.1   *Infernal Affairs III:* Lau on CCTV

Characters tune into images of themselves that rob them of their self-identity. For example, "honest" Wong becomes the corrupt conspirator when caught on video with Mary. Ngai describes this tape of Wong and Mary as an "awesome show." Four different grainy views of the hotel room come up on the monitor as Mary repeats, "I'm not blackmailing you. We've simply passed the point of no return" (Still 5.2). Ngai feels he has indisputable visual evidence of police culpability and expects the tape to bring Wong to justice. However, as in the case of the Los Angeles police who beat Rodney King on tape in 1991 and were acquitted the following year, Wong suffers little from being caught in the act other than a lengthy internal investigation in which he is eventually exonerated. The mechanically reproduced images on the screen lack legitimacy and substance. Flexible, these images can be controlled by the "occult powers" they mask and remade or discarded at will.

Still 5.2 *Infernal Affairs II:* video monitor

Beyond the insistent use of surveillance video throughout the trilogy, broadcast television acts as an important medium for the shaping of identity in *Infernal Affairs*. In *Infernal Affairs I*, broadcast news announces Wong's death, and, soon after, reports on the death of the undercover mole Keung. While Wong's death is a cold fact, Keung is far from a police mole, and the power of television to shape and misshape identities becomes a fact within the fiction.

The depiction of the handover in *Infernal Affairs II* provides a striking instance of the conflation of on-screen and off-screen personae with strong links to the rest of the trilogy's tacit commentary on Hong Kong politics as well as the postmodern crisis of identity. Speaking more generally, Stephen Teo notes:

> ... Hong Kong's type of postmodernism can thus be seen as a sign of a culture caught in the tension between a desire to construct a non-colonial identity by mobilising a sense of the past, and a profound anxiety about the possibility of that very identity being imposed rather than being constructed autonomously.[3]

The film presents the handover at midnight on June 30, 1997, as an event staged for television (Still 5.3). Intercut with the media event, the Hong Kong police — as individuals and in groups — change their insignia to conform to the televisual image (Still 5.4). Rain falling at police headquarters as well as at the site of the ceremony, the moment has a feeling of pathos coupled with a certain amount of speculation about the consequences of the

Still 5.3 *Infernal Affairs II:* handover on TV

Still 5.4 *Infernal Affairs II:* badge changes

passing of the colonial administration and the changing of the guard to Chinese sovereignty. The juxtaposition of the audio simulating media reportage with the visual image — sometimes showing fictional characters in the diegesis and sometimes showing the geopolitical actors on the historical platform staged for the media — provides a dialectical play between history as simulation and fiction as a mirror of historical change. *Infernal Affairs II* does not show the "reality" of the handover; rather, it presents a mass-mediated ceremonial image within a cinematic fiction meant to gesture toward the "reality" of individual lives behind the ceremonial change in sovereignty in which people are expected to change their identities in keeping with the change in political circumstances. Both are artificial simulations of a staged event that beg the question of "authenticity."

As the off-screen female voice from the television broadcast narrates the details of the handover ceremony:

> The handover ceremony of Hong Kong commenced earlier at 11:20. Both countries' anthems were played. A British flag rose up in the hall. The ceremony was dignified, but it had its share of

relaxed moments before its commencement. When both countries' marching bands played, some Chinese dignitaries took pictures. Prince Charles and Governor Patten were smiling. As the ceremony officially commenced, three British soldiers and three Chinese ones marched slowly to the podium. The Chinese soldiers displayed the PRC flag. Following their lead three HK police emerged with three HKSAR police officers. The three SAR officers displayed the HKSAR flag to the honorable guests. All the guests have risen. It was exactly midnight.

The characters in the fiction make their identities conform to the mass-mediated image. However, an ironic tinge clings to the images of their transformation. As the voice-over describes the rise of the British flag, SP Wong sits at his desk with still photographs of the massacred Ngai family. In his single-minded efforts to rid Hong Kong of the Ngai clan, he not only conspired to kill the patriarch Kwun, but he also became inextricably linked to the assassination of Ngai in Hong Kong and his entire family in Hawaii. The bloody corpses of the women and children in the family litter his desk under his miniature version of the British Union Jack. Wong replaces Ngai's photograph with Sam's on his board of triad criminals. The image ironically plays with the voice-over references to Chinese dignitaries taking pictures as Prince Charles and Governor Patten smile. As the representative of colonial power, Wong's own photographs of wanted criminals and dead children underscore the ambiguity of his supposedly "dignified" and legitimate power, since his actions led to the carnage. However, as the prince and the governor relinquish colonial authority, Wong maintains his position — bolstered by his being cleared of any wrongdoing for ordering the murder of Kwun and celebrated for overseeing the death of the hated triad boss Ngai.

When the announcement is made of the display of the PRC flag, Wong changes his insignia to the new SAR badge. As the voice-over describes the raising of the HKSAR flag, Wong fingers the crown on the old insignia. Ironically, the last change in Hong Kong's police badge occurred in 1969, two years after the bloody 1967 riots sparked by the Great Proletarian Cultural Revolution from across the border, in recognition of the force's handling of the crisis. After losing ten officers, the force was granted the designation "Royal" at that time to become the Royal Hong Kong Police Force (1969–97).[4] Moving from an honor conveyed because the force had successfully acted against the political tide coming from the PRC in support of British imperial authority, the new badge celebrates the force as an organ of the state returned to Chinese sovereignty and, ultimately, Communist Party rule.

Directly and indirectly implicated in two assassinations and a massacre, SP Wong does not leave colonial Hong Kong unsullied. At the moment of the handover, Wong represents the continuation of Hong Kong's "second system" within the "one country, two systems," and its legacy of ineffectual governance, lax administration, and corruption under the rubric of the "rule of law." Again, the casting of the biracial Anthony Wong in this role underscores this point as it is "written all over his face."

As the film intercuts shots of the changing of the flag at the police station within the fictional diegesis with television footage of the flag changing ceremony, Lau admires his new insignia in the mirror. The rise of the ethnic Chinese as symbols of PRC nationalism eager to replace a corrupt colonialism, however, remains a fiction as insubstantial as the image reflected in the mirror. Newly promoted, Lau mimics the role of model officer for the colonials, and the transition to Chinese sovereignty does nothing to disturb his cover. A shot of the televisized ceremony follows, and Lau's image as fake cop stands side-by-side with the artificial pomp on screen. The colonial flag has been replaced by the HKSAR Bauhinia within the fiction and within the mass-mediated footage of the handover ceremony. Lau salutes with the other officers wearing the new insignia, and the salute echoes his earlier (in the discourse)/later (in the story) salute under the PRC flag at Chan's grave in *Infernal Affairs I*. Flexible in his allegiance, Lau (played by Edison Chen in *II* and Andy Lau in *I*) has no difficulty changing face to fit in with new circumstances.

The quality of the sound changes with an increase in its apparent fidelity, and the voice no longer seems to be mediated by broadcast transmission:

> The arrival of July 1, 1997.The PRC flag with the HKSAR flag — marking the end of the colonial era; it also signified the beginning of the one country two systems policy. The Hong Kong Special Administrative Region of the People's Republic of China has been established.

The image shifts from Lau saluting with his new insignia to Sam at a window in front of the handover fireworks display. Sam looks at a photo of himself with Mary that parallels Wong's contemplation of the photographs of the murdered Ngai family at the beginning of the sequence. As mentioned in the above discussion of the scene, the moment conjures up a wealth of associations. Although festive and flamboyant from a European perspective, the white dinner jacket alludes to the funereal white worn by Chinese in mourning. The colors of the fireworks flicker red and blue on his face — calling up the infernal fires associated with the trilogy's title. Sam's face reflected in the window is doubled, and the theme of conflicted identities is visually linked to the handover as an oxymoronic festive loss and bleak celebration. When Sam bounds through the doors to toast the revelers with a full glass of brandy, he literally "puts on a happy face," and, symbolically, moves on with this new identity/ mask into the changed circumstances of the HKSAR.

Both Sam and Wong experience the handover with a sense of loss; i.e., Sam of his wife Mary and the memory of being loyal to his triad family and Wong of the colonial administration and his memory of being an honorable member of the force. Neither can return to the "good old days." However, both have survived the handover and must fashion an identity in keeping with the new regime. They manage, but it is Lau who embraces his new identity as an officer of the SAR with more of a smile than a tear and a grimace. Wong may rededicate himself to the pursuit of Sam as the new triad head and Sam may put on a grin as he greets July 1; however, Lau, as he did in his promotion hearing, articulates an opportunity and embodies the handover as a celebration of possibility. Given his affairs are "infernal," his optimism does not seem to suit his circumstances.

While Wong and Sam complicate the media representation of the handover, Lau illustrates it. Like the televised image of the changing of the guard at the official ceremony, Lau reflects the mass-produced simulation that stands in for the actual change of sovereignty. Standing outside of his own history as well as the history of Hong Kong, Lau has become the "control screen" of the moment — instantaneously registering his new identity as part of the transformation of Hong Kong. As such, he resembles Baudrillard's notion of the dissolution of the Cartesian subject into the postmodern schizophrenic:

> What characterizes him is less the loss of the real, the light years of estrangement from the real, the pathos of distance and radical separation, as is commonly said; but, very much to the contrary, the absolute proximity, the total instantaneity of things, the feeling of no defense, no retreat. It is the end of interiority and intimacy, the overexposure and transparence of the world which traverses him without obstacle. He can no longer produce the limits of his own being, can no longer play nor stage himself, can no longer produce himself as mirror. He is now only a pure screen, a switching center for all the networks of influence.[5]

Fredric Jameson, in a similar vein, discusses the postmodern schizophrenic's experience of the "the total instantaneity of things" as the ""undifferentiated vision of the world in the present."[6] No longer a subject of history, the postmodern schizophrenic has been subjected to the consequences of its loss.

Hell-Bent: The Psychoanalytic Encounter

In many ways, the depiction of the media's version of the handover in *Infernal Affairs II* tells a story about forgetting. As Fredric Jameson observes: "The informational function of the media would thus be to help us forget, to serve as the very agents and mechanisms for our historical amnesia."[7] This societal amnesia parallels the poor memory of the individual protagonists, who never seem to remember where they first met. As Yingchi Chu observes in *Hong Kong Cinema: Coloniser, Motherland, and Self,* memory loss has become a common trope in post-1997 cinema:

> Memory loss becomes a frequent narrative motif in the post-1997 films. Whether the 'past' is too 'difficult' to recall or too painful to remember, identity cannot be articulate without a past. Likewise, concealing one's 'past' is a rejection of one's present identity.[8]

Zhang Yingjin notes that forgetting functions as "a reminder of the unresolved question of identity and the future of Hong Kong."[9] When Chan and Lau first meet after the police academy, they have forgotten each other. They both struggle to forget their gangster origins throughout the trilogy — Chan tries to separate himself from the Ngai family, and Lau tries to rid himself of any association with Sam, bury the memory of his involvement with Mary's assassination, and move on with his life as a cop with his new Mary.

Throughout the trilogy, amnesia, uncertain identity, and the feminine intertwine.

From Tsai Chin's "Forgotten Times," the disembodied female voice has been privileged and marginalized, recognized and repressed in *Infernal Affairs*. Lau gets down on his knees in the presence of Tsai Chin's voice. Her voice marks the common ground of repression between Chan and Lau — and, more generally, the audience. Tsai Chin also links both Marys to Lau, and her voice becomes part of a series of female voices that shape the narrative. An anonymous woman provides the media's "voice of God" narration for Hong Kong's change in sovereignty and transformation of identity. In addition, Dr. Lee's therapeutic voice connects Chan and Lau's common search for affirmation of their respective identities. Although women do not play major dramatic roles in the trilogy, their voices define the relationships between characters and form the foundation for the thematic structure of the films.

As a female psychiatrist, the gendered figure of Dr. Lee underscores both Chan's and Lau's difficulties in reconciling their identities as men with the strictures of the patriarchy. Both rebel against their fathers/father figures. As the unhappy son of a triad kingpin, Chan spends his life trying to destroy his natal family. Ironically, in trying to obliterate the legacy of his gangster father, he comes to fill that same role. Just as his mother estranged herself from Kwun, Chan's love interests run from him — hiding or aborting his progeny to keep children away from a figure they see as a violent gangster. His outburst when he learns of the abortion in *Infernal Affairs II* concretizes his anger and frustration at his inability to forge a role as father separate from his own dysfunctional dad.

Lau has a similar problem, which mirrors Chan's. He wants to destroy his triad mentor Sam in order to possess Mary (a maternal figure, as her name implies by reference to the Christian Bible). Mary, however, rejects Lau and remains loyal to Sam, thus frustrating Lau's ambition to move ahead in the triads as well as his love life by taking Mary as his own. Although Lau may hint to Dr. Lee that the treacherous Mary seduced him into a life of crime, the misogynistic thought remains unsubstantiated by any overt act by Mary shown in the trilogy, and the fact his misguided obsession disqualifies him from the role of patriarch in either a criminal or a legitimate family remains on his shoulders. Even after Lau takes up with the second Mary, he never takes up the role of patriarch, and he ends up estranged from his wife and child. Chan's and Lau's failure to become patriarchs by founding their own families reverberates with their identity crises. This puts pressure on their functioning as men, and, in turn, their sanity (the very core of their being) comes into question. The representation of Chan and Lau as men in *Infernal Affairs* mirrors a more general "crisis" in masculinity in Hong Kong cinema. Although referring to the depiction of masculinity in films produced by the company Milkyway Image (often starring Andy Lau as the male "in crisis"), Laikwan Pang's remarks describe Chan and Lau equally well:

> ... male characters were often put under the spell of some omnipotent forces; slowly and brutally the male protagonists were made to struggle and look, often in vain, for ways out of their predicament. These films no longer exhibited male confidence and aggressiveness so often seen in earlier Hong Kong gangster and action movies. The man's world portrayed was full of anxiety and disturbance, and the characters were often in a state of insecurity and fear. Not only were they deprived of full confidence with regard to the opposite sex, but the relationships among the males were also often unsettled and complex. These films established a self-reflexive and intertextual world calling attention to a specific cinematic masculinity established in Hong Kong cinema, whose underlying mechanisms were revealed and problematized ... Women now embodied the future of Hong Kong.[10]

As one of the few major characters to survive, Dr. Lee becomes a pivotal figure in attempting to manage this crisis. On the government's payroll, she has been appointed by the courts to rehabilitate Chan through anger management therapy. The criminal justice system turns to psychiatry to fill voids in its execution of its mission. Dr. Lee represents a rational nod to the irrational basis of deviancy, and she makes a concerted, professional effort to do her job and "cure" Chan of his antisocial aggression. Unfortunately, like the representatives of most other organs of the state portrayed in the trilogy, Dr. Lee has been duped. Chan and Lau lie to her and use her to shore up their precarious identities as cops and crooks. Although both reveal their status as mole to her, it remains difficult to determine whether or not her skills as a psychiatrist had anything to do with it. In the case of Chan, his growing romantic attraction to Lee makes it difficult for him not to tell her he really is a "good guy" — i.e., a cop.[11] Similarly, Lau's precipitous psychotic breakdown makes it difficult for him to contain the fact he wants to destroy his identity as Sam's mole. Playing solitaire on the computer, Lee's hard work as an analyst remains mainly off-screen.

From *The Cabinet of Dr. Caligari* (1919) and *Secrets of the Soul* (1926) though Hitchcock's evocation of the profession in films like *Spellbound* (1945) and *Psycho* (1960) to the current pairing of psychiatrists with gangsters on screen in *Analyze This* (1999), *Analyze That* (2002), and *The Sopranos*, psychiatry — psychoanalysis in particular — has a long history of motion picture representation. Given that Sigmund Freud's work came to international prominence around the same time that film emerged as a medium of mass communication and entertainment, the fact that the two should share an overlapping history within the popular imagination should not come as a surprise. While the "mad doctor" using psychology in the service of crime and the psychiatrist as an "expert" on the mind of the criminal deviant have been standard screen fixtures for decades, the current positioning of psychiatry on the cusp of an ethical conundrum involving the dark side of capitalism embodied by the gangster provides a new twist on the old formulae. Without any prodding from the state, Tony Soprano, in the television series *The Sopranos*, goes into analysis to cure his anxiety, and Paul Vitti in *Analyze This* and *Analyze That* does the same. The gangsters are sincere, and they have faith that psychiatry will "cure" them. The psychiatrists must, however, remain on guard not to facilitate their patients' illegal enterprises.

Dr. Lee's analysis of Chan plays primarily as comedy-romance. From Lee's point of view, Chan displays behavior expected in a therapeutic relationship; i.e., he initially resists treatment, becomes attached to his therapist through transference, etc. However, Chan actually tries desperately to keep Lee away from his secret identity as a police mole. Most of this serves as comic respite as Chan toys with alarm clocks, eats crackers, sleeps in Lee's office, concocts outrageous stories about his past, and makes car deals during his sessions. It turns to romance when Chan professes his love for the doctor. Dr. Lee calls him "delusional" and attributes the attraction to transference, so Chan must turn to the buffoon Keung to find out what Dr. Lee means. Armed with information from *Reader's Digest*, Keung gives Chan a mini-lecture on psychoanalysis, Freud, hypnosis, trauma, and symbolic memories. However, Lee steps over the psychiatric — if not the generic — line, and she reciprocates Chan's affections. Eventually, Chan reveals his identity as a cop to her.

Although Lau appears to cultivate his relationship with Lee in order to keep tabs on any information Chan may have given her on his status as Sam's mole, he quickly takes his place on the couch as one of Dr. Lee's patients. While Chan moves from patient to lover, Lau metamorphoses from police protector to psycho on Lee's couch. A single scene links all three as morally culpable. Intercutting between Lau and Chan in Lee's office, *Infernal Affairs III* collapses time, so that Chan and Lau appear to share a single analytic session with Lee (Stills 5.5 and 5.6). Lee begins by telling her own story about being a thief, liar, and snitch. Feeling she may be caught for stealing candy, Lee as a young girl accused a store manager of molestation. For some unknown reason, the manager never revealed Lee's lie, and she only admitted the false accusation much later to a college friend. Returning to the theme of justice and the circulation of information about crime, *Infernal Affairs III* continues to question the morality of being an informant. In this case, Lee falsely informs on the store manager in an attempt to save her own skin, paralleling Chan's and Lau's operation as moles. They work as snitches to keep their own skin intact. They serve as pawns in a game that has led to a stalemate. While Lee's statement that revealing her secret made her "feel like a newborn," it did little in the service of justice. Similarly, Chan's opening up about his work as an undercover cop and Lau's revelation that he serves as Sam's mole in the police force do not lead to any closure in the narrative.

Still 5.5   *Infernal Affairs III:* Lau on the couch

Still 5.6   *Infernal Affairs III:* Chan on the couch

Rather, psychiatry, like all the other operations of the state in *Infernal Affairs*, proves to be ineffective. Chan seems right when he says: "You can't help me. My job is to betray folks around me." Lau appears to continue Chan's thought in the same sequence: "I

don't know when I can stop. To survive I have to betray others."
They recognize, like Lee, their actions have defined them, and they
are both trapped. The focus shifts in Lee's story from a question of
morality (i.e., of stealing, lying, and snitching) to one of identity
(i.e., of feeling like a "newborn"). For Chan and Lau, whether the
police or triads are more corrupt no longer makes any difference,
since betrayal has moved from a question of morality to a definition
of identity. They experience an existential crisis — to exist, they
must betray others. While therapeutic discourse freed Lee from a
childhood trauma, it does little for either Chan or Lau. Psychiatry,
as an institutional branch of the state, cannot cure the malaise at
the heart of the postmodern crisis of identity. As Fredric Jameson
notes:

> ... from this nostalgic and regressive perspective — that of the
> older modern and its temporalities — what is mourned is the
> memory of deep memory; what is enacted is a nostalgia for
> nostalgia, for the grand older extinct questions of origin and telos,
> of deep time and the Freudian Unconscious (dispatched by
> Foucault in one blow in the *History of Sexuality*), for the dialectic
> also, as well as all the monumental forms left high and dry by the
> ebb tide of the modern moment, forms whose Absolutes are no
> longer audible to us, illegible hieroglyphs of the demiurgic within
> the technocratic world.
>
> ... memory has been weakened in our time, and that the great
> rememberers are a virtually extinct species: for us, memory, when
> it is a strong experience and still able to testify to the reality of
> the past, only serves to annihilate time and that past along with
> it.[12]

Neither Chan nor Lau has much faith in the cliché Dr. Lee lives by
that "the truth will set you free," and it makes sense that Dr. Lee
seems to spend as much time in the police graveyard mourning as
she does in the office. She represents nostalgia for "Forgotten

Times," but the recovery of memory does not "cure" her patients or comfort her for her own loss.

However, although they share the same analytic bed, Lau and Chan offer very different models of this crisis. In *Anti-Oedipus: Capitalism and Schizophrenia,* Gilles Deleuze and Félix Guattari state with confidence:

> A schizophrenic out for a walk is a better model than a neurotic lying on the analyst's couch. A breath of fresh air, a relationship with the outside world.[13]

Infernal Affairs proffers a meditation on the relationship between the neurotic (Chan) and the schizophrenic (Lau) within the postmodern condition. The trilogy presents Chan as a bundle of neurotic symptoms. Before his tapping finger becomes associated with his Morse code communications with Wong, Chan's incessant tapping appears to be an uncontrollable neurotic symptom of anxiety. He often directly expresses his feelings of anxiety to Wong. He has clearly been traumatized, and he complains about being beaten up and abused by both cops and triads as he works undercover. He expresses guilt and shame over his life as a snitch, and he vents his feelings through violent behavior. The trilogy presents Lau, on the other hand, as clearly psychotic with little contact with any sense of "reality."

Schizophrenia aptly describes this character's apparent state of mind. Lau suffers delusions (beginning with the projection of his unrequited erotic feelings onto Sam's wife Mary) and hallucinations (from his own version of the exchange on the rooftop with Chan to his encounters with the dead Chan, Wong, and Mary). Eventually, he can no longer string a coherent identity together from one moment to the next, and he ends up thinking he is Chan out to arrest himself/Lau. Lau's writer wife Mary imagines her fictional hero (based on Lau) as suffering from multiple personality disorder. Lau's hallucinations and delusions point to the schizophrenic's loss of boundaries and general incoherence and inability to function. He has split apart and, by the denouement of *Infernal Affairs III*, he has channeled the dead Chan into the only part of his body that can still move independently — i.e., his tapping finger. If not clear earlier, it becomes quite apparent by this point that Lau has molded himself to fit in with the various roles he has been assigned throughout the trilogy from triad mole to upright cop to devoted husband and father. If the neurotic can cling to a unified sense of self and a belief in an outside reality from which he can be distinguished as a separate individual, the schizophrenic embodies the opposite extreme in which identity is in constant flux, multiple, incoherent, fragmentary, contradictory, malleable, and illusory. From a Lacanian perspective, the schizophrenic cannot position himself as an "I" in discourse in order to string a sentence together. Lau, the schizophrenic, has swallowed Chan, the neurotic.

Infernal Affairs visually reinforces Lau's schizophrenia by providing several shots in which Lau gazes back at his fragmented self-image. In *Infernal Affairs I*, a brief shot shows the younger Lau gazing into a security mirror at a convenience store (Still 5.7). Later, this moment takes on significance as the image is repeated in *Infernal Affairs II* and revealed to be the moment when Lau looks at himself after he has made the phone call that will lead to Mary's assassination. Again, combining the paranoia of surveillance with a sense of Lau as deeply divided character, a similar shot shows Lau staring at his own image in a CCTV monitor in an elevator on his way to the internal hearing in *Infernal Affairs III*. Lau, aware he is being scrutinized, seems to have his own surveillance under control as the elevator conjures up his murder of Billy in an elevator in which Lau had sabotaged the closed circuit television. All of these reflections frame Lau as a murderer, but they also divide him as he looks at himself in the shiny surface of his police badge and sees a cop or looks at himself in the mirror and sees Chan smiling back.

As Baudrillard notes, the mirror has given way as a reflecting surface to the non-reflecting surface of the television screen and computer monitor: "In place of the reflexive transcendence of mirror and scene, there is a nonreflecting surface, an immanent surface where operations unfold — the smooth operational surface of communication."[14] Technology defines the schizophrenic as the norm.

Still 5.7   *Infernal Affairs II:* Lau in the mirror

In addition to Jameson and Baudrillard, many commentators on the postmodern condition have noted the "crisis" of the Cartesian subject and the appearance of the "schizophrenic" in place of the rational, bourgeois, unified ego. However, other scholars involved with feminist, postcolonial, queer, ethnic, or other studies of "difference" have pointed out that the unified, self-determining, self-defined, and self-contained ego never really defined "identity" for those who did not fit within a narrow white, heterosexual, male, bourgeois frame.[15] Women have engaged in the "feminine masquerade."[16] Blacks operate with a "double consciousness" with "black skin" under "white masks."[17] Gays, lesbians, and others outside of the heterosexual norm too often find themselves "in the closet" with a dual identity.[18] Working class ethnics must learn to speak, dress, and comport themselves one way to be upwardly mobile, while maintaining a separate argot, costume, religion/value system, and lifestyle in order to remain connected to their "roots" and not completely ostracized by their natal community. The colonial subject has always had to "mimic" the colonizer, while doomed forever to being not "quite" right (white) as an imitation.[19]

However, within postmodernity, the "model" identity, the "norm" of an earlier historical moment has begun to take on traces of what had been the condition of the oppressed; i.e., fragmented identity, deracination, multiple masks, etc. While the notion of an "authentic" identity of a matriarchal prehistory, a pre-colonial past, or an imagined classless future fuels the hope for liberation with a dream of utopia for the oppressed, this fiction, too, has been under assault within postmodernity. In fact, in hindsight, the solidity of the Eurocentric bourgeois ego of the Enlightenment — for both the powerful and oppressed — begins to melt away into fiction as a construction of an emergent capitalism, nationalism, and colonialism within global modernity.

Within postmodern culture, it becomes easier for characters suffering through the identity "crisis" of colonialism and its aftermath to stand in for a more general "crisis" in subjectivity.[20] Identities can be created and recreated through the consumption of commodities, rebuilt with cybernetic implants, hidden within the anonymity of cyberspace, disembodied and reconfigured instantaneously via satellite beams, and hybridized and transported across borders through jet travel (Still 5.8). Lau, even with a gun at his head, fits the bill as the postmodern chameleon — tuning in the satellite signal of the moment, slipping between "good guy" and "bad guy," lacking any sense of a moral, ethical, national, or ethnic "center." He builds himself up through commodities like stereos, watches, cell phones, computers, and clothes, and he sees it as his right to erase his personal history and recreate himself at will.

Still 5.8   *Infernal Affairs:* Lau and Chan with satellite

In many ways, the colonial/postcolonial state has created its own monster in the form of the fragmented Lau. In *Infernal Affairs II*, Lau's interview in English to determine his suitability for promotion within the force, a mentioned earlier, provides a telling example. He has absorbed the Western bourgeois values of individualism, and he does not hesitate to express his self-confidence to the panel. A split colonial subject, he can easily express an ego associated with "leadership" and "belief" in himself and his own abilities in English that can coexist with a separate persona as a triad underling devoted to his "big brother" in Cantonese. He passes this internal hearing with flying colors, and, a few scenes later, also "passes" Sam's test of loyalty by organizing his escape from police protection.

As John Berger points out in *Ways of Seeing*,[21] to-be-looked-at-ness feminizes the object of the gaze, and the more Lau becomes the object of others' scrutiny the more he loses the agency associated with his masculinity. Indeed, the female characters are the ones who take a good look at Lau and force him into his psychotic breakdown. In *Infernal Affairs I*, Lau's wife Mary suspects her husband has a secret identity, and the tape of Sam's conversation with Lau confirms the worst for her. In *Infernal Affairs II*, Sam's wife Mary takes a good look at her sexual assailant and murderer before Uncle John from the Ngai family runs her down and kills her. In *Infernal Affairs III*, the close up of Dr. Lee's startled face when Lau reveals he has worked as Sam's mole also registers Lau's identity.

The castrating gaze of the female other traps Lau, immobilizes him, defines him as an evil gangster, and gives him an identity from which he cannot escape. Although the film continues, Lau's story ends with him paralyzed in a wheelchair trapped between images of the two Marys. Lau's wife Mary wearing a red coat visits him on the lawn of the institution's grounds. Even though he does not move about, schizophrenic Lau does get Deleuze and Guattari's "breath of fresh air." In the space behind Lau, Sam's wife Mary, dressed in a black leather coat, stands on the open grass (Still 5.9). She pulls out a gun, aims it at Lau, and fires. Lau just slightly turns his head. Returning his attention to his wife Mary in front of him, he listens to his wife report that "the baby can say 'papa.'" She then walks away (Still 5.10). Mary, raising her daughter as a single mother, and Mary, who exacts revenge on her killer (if only in his fevered imagination), finally put the mole Lau to rest as a threat.

Still 5.9   *Infernal Affairs III:* Lau with Mary

Still 5.10   *Infernal Affairs III:* Lau with Mary

The camera moves from Lau's smile down to a close shot of his finger tapping on the edge of wheelchair. The fact that the camera moves, while Lau can barely lift a finger, underscores the power of the cinema image and the impotence of the character. *Infernal Affairs* leaves Lau incapacitated, helpless, with masochistic delusions of self-destruction, and a pathetic identification with his nemesis Chan. The fact his daughter can say "papa" only drives the point home that he does not function as the potent patriarch of the family, but sits as a shattered, castrated reminder that his active, masculine, heterosexual identity shattered when he lost his police badge.

Lau has been placed in a passive position, feminized and sandwiched between two women, almost immobile, and left as an observer/object of the camera's gaze. However, not only does this make it easier for the film viewers — seated immobile in the cinema (as "feminized" masses)[22] — to see themselves in and enjoy looking at Lau, it also smoothes the transition to the trilogy's final image. Bryan Chang, for example, analyzes this moment in relation to Lau's screen persona and star appeal as follows:

> ... he sits on a wheelchair like an undead. Sammi Cheng and Carina Lau, like little riding hood in red and the bride who wore black, are no longer hurting. They are instead comforting the wild wolf who can no longer move. As if Lau Kin-ming is living in our memory forever, this is an image of eternal youth, as I fondly retain the past qualities of immaturity, restlessness, inferiority and self-satisfaction, flamboyant ... My (kind of) Andy Lau moment.[23]

In the last scene, Lau reappears in the past, "Forgotten Times" plays on the soundtrack, and Lau's final close-up freezes him as a happy consumer. In fact, the final close-up seems to sum up the culture of surveillance and consumerism that forms the bedrock of the trilogy (Still 5.11). Moving from surveillance based on the needs

Still 5.11   *Infernal Affairs III:* Lau in stereo store

of the state (the police) and the capitalist (the drug runners), the film shifts to what Mark Poster, taking his cue from Michel Foucault,[24] has called the "Superpanoptican," in which "individuals are constituted as consumers and participants in the disciplining and surveillance of themselves as consumers."[25] Lau has reconciled himself with being an object of surveillance as the model consumer as well as screen star. Everything may fall apart within postmodernity — historical, ethnic, national, gender, and sexual identities — but the power of consumerism and the joys of shopping stand out from linear chronology, identity crises, and the fires of hell. Lau the performer takes over from Lau the character as a guarantor of customer satisfaction. Lau the star triumphs — frozen in time as a screen icon and model of consumerism.[26]

The Devil's Masquerade: Performance and Star Power

Given its plot dealing with a cop acting the part of a crook and a triad playing the role of a cop, *Infernal Affairs* highlights the idea of performance as an element of its narrative. The trilogy is about taking up masks and the difficulty of wearing these constructed identities. In fact, the plot explicitly deals with the search for a "genuine" subjectivity, the fiction of that notion of identity, and the consequences of performing that fiction. Slavoj Zizek remarks:

> The path to an authentic subjective position runs therefore "from the outside inward": first, we pretend to be something, we just act as if we are that, till, step by step, we actually become it ... The performative dimension at work here consists of the symbolic efficiency of the 'mask': wearing a mask actually *makes us* what we feign to be ... the only authenticity at our disposal is that of impersonation, of "taking our act (posture) seriously."[27]

The trilogy deals with characters who must take their act very seriously and with actors who must perform the role of performers diligently in order to drag their work out of the box office doldrums. Thus, much of the film relies on playing with and against star image as well as playing the actors' performances against a narrative based on deceit and hidden identities. Screen persona, personality, and star image operate together to create a fantasy with local as well as global appeal. However, as Dorinne Kondo warns, these performative identities must never be considered to be occasioned by the whims of "free" individuals:

> Performative citations are thus never merely the voluntary choices of a humanist subject; rather, they are the product of constitutive constraints that create identities, creative performances elicited under duress.[28]

Infernal Affairs brings together a production package featuring many of Hong Kong's most established stars, recognized character actors, and promising new talent. Although they fit together into a coherent dramatic ensemble, the performers each bring a different style and public persona to the trilogy. A significant part of the energy of the films comes from the pairings of actors — e.g., Tony Leung and Andy Lau, Tony Leung and Anthony Wong, Eric Tsang and Anthony Wong, Tony Leung and Chapman To, Tony Leung and Kelly Chen, Andy Lau and Sammi Cheng, Anthony Wong and Hu Jun, Edison Chen and Carina Lau, Andy Lau and Leon Lai, Eric Tsang and Chen Daoming, etc. However, although these dramatic pairings form an important element of the trilogy's plot, they do not rest on a uniform acting style.

In fact, since the characters self-consciously play roles in the film and hide other identities, the fact that the actors often appear not to "be" in the scene in which they find themselves makes perfect dramatic sense. For example, in many of the scenes between Sammi

Cheng/Mary and Andy Lau/Lau Kin-ming, Lau appears to be distracted, elsewhere, and not quite able to interact with Cheng. This characterization of their onscreen relationship, of course, reaches its natural conclusion in *Infernal Affairs III* in the sanitarium in which the paralyzed Lau barely reacts to Cheng/ Mary's presence.

Although positioned between the action genres of the *policier* and the gangster film, *Infernal Affairs* primarily presents its story through relationships rather than action. Established through patterns of looking and being looked at, pursuing and being pursued, lurking in the shadows and stepping out into the light of day, performances mainly revolve around observing and being observed rather than acting and reacting. Throughout their screen careers, Tony Leung and Andy Lau have perfected this type of screen performance. In *Cinema 2*, Gilles Deleuze describes this acting style as an outgrowth of the crisis in post-World War II film culture:

> A new type of character for a new cinema. It is because what happens to them does not belong to them and only half concerns them, because they know how to extract from the event the part that cannot be reduced to what happens: the part of inexhaustible possibility that constitutes the unbearable, the intolerable, the visionary's part. A new type of actor was needed: not simply the non-professional actors that neo-realism had revived at the beginning, but what might be called professional non-actors, or, better, actor-mediums, capable of seeing and showing rather than acting, and either remaining dumb or undertaking some never-ending conversation, rather than of replying or following a dialogue ...[29]

Although the pairing of actors becomes an important part of the performance landscape of *Infernal Affairs*, the fact that the two stars remain aloof, observing rather than fully participating in the action, also provides an important cinematic element. The scene in the stereo store sets the tone — Chan/Leung and Lau/Lau listen and enjoy another performance by Tsai Chin. They sit side by side on display for the film audience to be observed and to take in what is in the environment that surrounds them. In fact, their bodies become fixtures in an environment, elements of the mise-en-scène, able to "channel" their performance rather than "act" a role that must convince the audience of unified and coherent character seamlessly impersonated by a "method" actor.

While action, movement, progress, and change characterize the "modern" subject, postmodernity, as Jean Baudrillard notes, places the subject in front of the television screen or computer monitor; the subject may experience the speed of sounds and images occupying the mind, but the body remains still. Deleuze also points out that, during the post-war era's "crisis" in cinema, cameras began to move more independently of characters, so that the camera gaze became more mobile as characters became more fixed in place. In fact, this is one of Andrew Lau's signature cinematographic tropes, and several scenes in the trilogy feature tableaux that seem to freeze the characters in mid-action. The gathering at the police station in which the gangsters and officers stand still while Sam eats in *Infernal Affairs I*, the toast led by Ngai to his dead father in *Infernal Affairs II*, and the end of most movement with the discovery of the recording of "Forgotten Times" in *Infernal Affairs III* provide just a few examples.

Although not all motion stops, the movement of characters becomes minimal, creating a tableau effect. Of course, these tableaux also showcase the presence of the stars by bringing some of the highest paid and most popular talent in Asia on screen within a single shot. At other points in the trilogy, the mise-en-scène remains static while the camera springs to life to investigate and move freely through screen space. As in the case of Lau in his wheelchair, the actor/character remains fixed, while the camera, the machinery of the cinema, takes up the action. At other moments, as with the final shot of the trilogy, the freeze frame close up delivers up the static image of the star as a new kind of "money shot," a rationalization of the price of admission by confirming the value of the star image.

Andy Lau won Taiwan's 2004 Golden Horse award for Best Actor for *Infernal Affairs III*. He had been nominated for the Golden Horse the year before for *Infernal Affairs*, and he was also nominated for Best Actor in the 2003 Hong Kong Film Awards for *Infernal Affairs*. In fact, he has been nominated for Best Actor awards on several occasions throughout his career, and he won the 2004 Hong Kong Film Best Actor Award for *Running on Karma* and the same award in 2000 for *Running Out of Time* — both times under the direction of Johnnie To. However, in spite of his box office popularity, his established success in television and film, and a lucrative career as a Cantopop star, Lau has been criticized for his wooden performances and lack of acting skill. In fact, Li Cheuk-to seems apologetic in his introduction to the catalogue that accompanied the 2005 Hong Kong International Film Festival tribute to Lau's screen career:

> Why Andy Lau? Many a friend who has asked this question does so with a deeply ingrained prejudice. With someone so famous and idolized as Andy Lau, the general assumption is that his acting is not something that could pass muster ... even if Andy Lau does not belong to the same school as Tony Leung Chiu-wai or Anthony Wong, we cannot simply just write him off.[30]

Although given the role of the sinister schizophrenic Lau Kin-ming who acts the role of the model cop and undergoes a psychotic breakdown, Lau needs to go a step further and perform the meatier role in the trilogy as the consumable star who models an image of consumption for the audience. Given that he is the government's spokesman for fair business practices to promote consumer confidence, he seems to be the perfect candidate for this role. In fact, Lau has played on his public image as the "face" of Hong Kong in the satiric *Golden Chicken* (2002) and *Golden Chicken II* (2003) in which he portrays "Andy Lau" as a televisual presence. In the former, he directly addresses the eponymous prostitute from the television screen to encourage her to provide the best service possible for her customers, and, in the sequel, he returns to make a television appearance as the HKSAR's last Chief Executive in the year 2046. In both films, he serves as the not so "authentic" voice of an imaginary Hong Kong, where consumerism, screen fantasy, and star power are the foundations of Hong Kong's "legitimate" identity.

In fact, Lau's roots in television as part of TVB prepared him well for this role of "professional non-actor." Tony Leung also emerged from the same TVB training program, and both performers share a common approach to "non-acting." Televisual rather than cinematic, Lau and Leung are masters of surface, flexible performers able to move from commercial endorsements (e.g., Lau drinks the bottled ice tea he promotes in commercials on screen in *Infernal Affairs*) to the art cinema non-actor "capable of seeing and showing rather than acting," as Deleuze has said.

Just as Andrew Lau positions his cinematic style somewhere between MTV and Wong Kar-wai, Andy Lau and Tony Leung appear to be very comfortable with performing fragmented roles, incoherent and abstruse characters, their bodies shredded across time and space, and their psyches crafted out of computer monitors, cell phones, and CCTV surveillance. Interrupted by commercials, broken up into weekly episodes, subject to redundancy for narrative coherence, television requires a very different approach to performance than cinema. Surface becomes more important than depth, and performers need to be more in tune with Baudrillard's schizophrenic fused with the small screen than with the emotional depths (and neuroses) of cinema's method actor or larger-than-life screen hero. Given that *Infernal Affairs* deals with the surfaces of identity, the fragmentation of the self, and the seductive appeal of the image, televisual performance styles work well for both Tony Leung and Andy Lau.

Referring to their days at TVB, Andy Lau talks about the way he and his colleagues like Tony Leung crafted their small screen personae by imitating Hollywood stars:

> Back then, Chou Yun-fat was Robert De Niro and Tony Leung Chiu-wai was Al Pacino. Tony Leung was so good at being Al Pacino already that there was no need to put in four or five times the effort to match him. If I wanted to find a route for myself, then I'll have to find something new.
>
> The important thing is to understand yourself and your opponent. Robert De Niro and Al Pacino were not considered handsome. But they were known to be good actors. No one said Marlon Brando was a good actor, but he was handsome. And that suits me well (laughs).[31]

In addition to continuing a "battle of the stars" between Lau and Leung that had been going on since the beginning of their careers in Hong Kong television, *Infernal Affairs* also continues a dialogue between the two media — televisual performance styles compete with stage/cinema techniques associated with the Method. Both Lau and Leung act the part of method actors acting the roles of gangsters who, in turn, often draw their deviant style from Hollywood. Their "authenticity" in performance is based on multiple layers of influence and conscious imitation.

Although carefully scripted, *Infernal Affairs* has that spontaneous quality associated with television's peripatetic camera and editing in tune with Lau and Leung's performance styles. Moreover, like studio television, some of the film was shot with multiple camera set-ups. As television's "non-actors" like Lau and Leung moved into the cinema under the tutelage of directors like Wong Kar-wai, their performance styles went with them. Tony

Leung, in particular, has been closely associated with Wong Kar-wai for many years, and his acting style rooted in TVB and developed with Wong forms the basis for his performance of Chan in *Infernal Affairs*. Unlike Lau, however, Leung has won more prestigious international accolades for his performances: Best Actor at Taiwan's 2003 Golden Horse Awards for *Infernal Affairs*; the same prize for *Infernal Affairs* from the Hong Kong Film Awards the same year; 1994 Best Actor at the Golden Horse for Wong Kar-wai's *Chungking Express*; and, Best Actor at the Hong Kong Film Awards for *Chungking Expresss, Happy Together, In the Mood for Love*, and *2046* — all directed by Wong Kar-wai. His most prestigious award came for *In the Mood for Love* (2002) at Cannes.

Unlike Lau and Mak, Wong tends to work without a script, and he often keeps his actors in the dark about their characters and even the basic operations of the film plot during shooting. Given the number of often contradictory versions of the same story shot at the same time, Wong's shooting schedules tend to be excessive, and production can drag on for years. Although this seems to be the opposite of the commercial Hong Kong (and Hollywood) norm and light years away from television's quick production schedules, this approach actually owes more to a televisual sense of temporality (long takes, repetition, interruption) than to cinema's more rigid adherence to scripts, specific camera angles, and careful blocking. Without a script, spontaneity and improvisation become possible, and, without clearly defined characters, "acting" becomes free from trying to create a unified, coherent, believable individual on screen. Memorizing lines and engaging in dialogue become secondary. Seeing and being seen take the place of acting and reacting. Clearly, Hou Hsiao-Hsien was also attracted to Leung's talent for professional "non-acting" when he cast him as the mute photographer, the observer of the transition from Japanese colonial Taiwan to the Republic of China on Taiwan, in *City of Sadness* (1989).

Leung brings the same performance qualities to *Infernal Affairs*. In many ways, Chan resembles the characters Leung has created in collaboration with Wong Kar-wai. Beginning with a cameo at the end of *Days of Being Wild* (1991), Leung's work with Wong has continued to highlight the casual gesture, inactivity, interiority, and observation. The lovelorn cop in *Chungking Express* perhaps best exemplifies Leung's approach to this type of character. Rather than taking action, he broods and remains rooted in place when his air hostess girlfriend leaves him. Absorbed in details, he notices that small things change in his apartment; however, he cannot seem to see that another woman Faye (Faye Wong) has taken control of his living space and is physically changing his life. Depressed, incapacitated, observant but not perceptive, he remains still, while the frenetic world of Hong Kong swirls around him. The cinematography reinforces Leung's performance by featuring him nearly still in the frame while the world around him appears to fly by in accelerated motion. While generic conventions demand the police take action, Leung has transformed this character into the "eye" at the center of the storm of contemporary urban life.

The importance of sight and its loss becomes the defining characteristic for Leung's character of a swordsman going blind, fated never to see his wife again, in *Ashes of Time* (1994).[32] In *Happy Together* (1997), Leung as Lai Yiu-fai again suffers from depression and incapacitation during the disintegration of his homosexual relationship with his lover Ho Po-wing (Leslie Cheung), who leaves and returns to him only to leave again.[33] As Chow Mo-wan in *In the Mood for Love* (2000), Leung again plays a character imprisoned by his own passivity, who loses his wife to another man and remains unable to consummate his love for the new woman in his life, Su Li-zhen (Maggie Cheung). Although this character becomes a more active lothario in the sequel *2046* (2004), Chow Mo-wan, as played by Leung, remains very much on the outside of life as a writer observing and imagining a world in which he has only limited involvement.

Although Leung has played a range of characters throughout his career and has seen his share of film action, his most memorable performances feature characters who remain on the sidelines as observers caught up in the machinations of others — witnesses to events over which the characters have little control. In *Infernal Affairs*, Chan becomes enmeshed in the plots of others, and he takes little action himself. Instead, he remains subject to the commands of SP Wong, Sam, and even Keung. Even though he plays a violent character who needs anger management therapy, Leung seldom takes action on screen. Rather, the violent outbursts are played by Shawn Yue or else take place off-screen. For example, *Infernal Affairs III* begins after Chan has finished fighting in the bathhouse, so that the battle remains unseen. One of the few instances in which Chan, played by Leung, takes action in the trilogy occurs when Sam orders Chan to attack Liang with an ashtray in the steakhouse in *Infernal Affairs III*. Again, this attack only comes under orders from Sam, and Chan has no idea why he has been asked to assault Liang. While the motives for the violence that takes place around Chan are quite clear, Chan cannot understand why he fights, and he becomes part of the absurdity that underlies so much of the world he inhabits. In this respect, Leung, because of his association with depressed, incapacitated, and passive characters in his work with Wong Kar-wai, easily slips into this hellish and absurd world in which he becomes embroiled in violent actions he cannot understand.

Although he originally wanted to play Chan as a smiling optimist and he does hit on that aspect of the character a bit in *Infernal Affairs III*, Leung has said that he ended up playing the character as "flat as I could ... I tried just to be quiet."[34] This stillness and flatness enable Leung to "channel" Chan in all his complexity as an emblem of a crisis in masculine potency, a generic type able to spout clichés like "everything will be fine" without crossing the line into parody, and a screen presence with bankable star quality.

Throughout their careers, all the principals in *Infernal Affairs* played the same type of roles they take on in the trilogy. Tony Leung, for example, has played police officers, undercover operatives, and gangsters on several occasions. He began his film career with a role in *Young Cops* (1985), and he switches to the other side of the law for Derek Yee's *People's Hero* (1987). Leung's work with John Woo — e.g., *Bullet in the Head* (1990) and *Hard Boiled* (1992) — has also had him embroiled in the underworld on both sides of the law. In fact, in *Hard Boiled*, he plays an undercover cop in the middle of a gang war — a role similar, in many respects, to Chan in *Infernal Affairs*. He portrays a poetic gangster based in Saigon/Ho Chi Minh City in *Cyclo* (1995) and a corrupt Macau cop working for the triads in Patrick Yau's *The Longest Nite* (1997).

Since his days in television, Andy Lau played cops and crooks — occasionally, as in *Lee Rock* and *Infernal Affairs*, both within the same film. He has been part of the criminal underworld in films like *Rich and Famous* (1987) and *Tragic Hero* (1987). Like Tony Leung, Andy Lau's work with Wong Kar-wai, although less extensive than Leung's, has helped to shape his career. His role as Tide in Wong's *Days of Being Wild* (1991) solidified his screen image. Also, his earlier portrayal of the gangster Wah in *As Tears Go By* (1988) helped to define not only Lau as an actor, but also Andrew Lau as a cinematographer. Lau plays a split character involved in the underworld at night while an exchange student by day in Ann Hui's *Zodiac Killers* (1991). He has been embroiled in underworld crime stories as diverse as *Casino Raiders* (1989), *Shanghai Grand* (1996), *A True Mob Story* (1998), *Running Out of Time* (1999), *A Fighter's Blues* (2000), and *Fulltime Killer* (2001).

Leon Lai also honed his acting skills working with Wong Kar-wai in *Fallen Angels* (1995). He plays a former cop who is the victim of a criminal mastermind in *Heroic Duo* (2003), which also stars

Francis Ng. However, Lai is probably best known for his starring role in *Comrades: Almost a Love Story*. Although he plays neither cop nor crook in this film, Lai does play a survivor, a PRC émigré, on the edges of Hong Kong and New York society. As in *Infernal Affairs III*, Lai specializes in roles in which he seems to stand outside society as a disgruntled assassin, a cop who is a convicted criminal, or a working class immigrant. Because of the divided nature of the characters he has previously portrayed in Hong Kong cinema, the fact that Yeung in *Infernal Affairs III* actually commits crimes and seems to be fundamentally corrupt, while turning out to be on the "right" side of the law in the end, does not take him far from the type of role with which he has been associated.

In *Infernal Affairs II*, Francis Ng plays Ngai as a type of gangster who bases his persona on Al Pacino's construction of Michael Corleone as the American-born, postwar, "modern" gangster. His performance is an allusion to another actor's meditation on how gangsters take up particular personae in order to create a public presence to solidify their power. Like Leung and Lau, Ng got his start through TVB's actor training program. He has often played the gangster in films such as *Once Upon a Time in a Triad Society* (1996) and its sequel, *Too Many Ways to Be Number One* (1997), as well as *The Mission* (1999), for which he won best actor at Taiwan's 2000 Golden Horse Awards. He stars in the triad tale *A War Named Desire* (2000) directed and co-written by *Infernal Affairs* co-director and co-writer Alan Mak. Francis Ng worked with Andrew Lau on *Young and Dangerous* (1996) and its prequel (1997) as Ugly Kwan — a triad role in a series that established Ng's screen image and made Andrew Lau a viable commercial filmmaker.

Anthony Wong has also had a substantial Hong Kong screen career playing cops and crooks. Like his co-stars, Wong began his acting career in television (first at ATV then TVB).[35] Also, like Andy Lau, Wong has a music career — but in rock and roll rather than

Cantopop music. He won the 1993 Hong Kong Film Award for best actor for his role in *The Untold Story* (1992) based on the actual case of a Macau man who had murdered several people and chopped them up to make pork buns out of them. In addition to showing the details of the killings, the film also shows the brutal treatment of the murderer at the hands of the Macau police.[36] The scene in *Infernal Affairs III* in which SP Wong sees Chan's broken body after he has been beaten by Yeung's team resonates with Wong's earlier role in *The Untold Story*, since he seems to have "been there" before as a victim of police brutality. Anthony Wong plays Tung who bridges both sides of the law in Gordon Chan and Dante Lam's *Beast Cops* (1998), and he won the 1999 Hong Kong Film Award for best actor for that role. Thus, the revelation that SP Wong is literally in bed with the triads comes as less of a shock to audiences familiar with Anthony Wong's screen career.

In addition to working as screenwriter, director, and producer, Eric Tsang has had a long screen career as a character actor, and he has played his share of triad and police roles. Although often playing cops and crooks for laughs, *Infernal Affairs* is not his first foray into drama. In addition to playing the Taiwanese gangster in Peter Chan's *Comrades: Almost a Love Story*, he worked with the same director on *Alan and Eric: Between Hello and Goodbye* (1991), and Tsang won the 1992 Hong Kong Film Award for best actor as the doomed character in a love triangle. Although not a crime film, it did allow Tsang to expand beyond comedy into more dramatic roles. He also won the Golden Horse Award for best supporting actor playing a gay character in Stanley Kwan's *Hold You Tight* (1997).

The younger actors in the trilogy are also screen veterans — e.g., Canadian-born Edison Chen in *Gen-X Cops* (2000), Shawn Yue in *Just One Look* (2001). Chapman To brings his gregarious persona from the radio to the screen in the trilogy. In addition to Andy Lau, Elva Hsiao, and Anthony Wong, several of the other performers in the film have substantial singing careers, including Tony Leung, Kelly Chen, Edison Chen, Sammi Cheng, and Leon Lai. Andy Lau has a long screen history with Sammi Cheng that helps flesh out their sketchy relationship by providing some intertextual romantic context — e.g., *Needing You* (2000), *Love on a Diet* (2001). Similarly, Carina Lau's long association with Wong Kar-wai in films such as *Days of Being Wild*, *Ashes of Time*, and *2046*, as well as off-screen relationship with Tony Leung, place her within the same milieu as the other performers in the trilogy.

Hu Jun may have one of the more interesting intertextual associations in the trilogy, since he previously played the PRC police officer who interrogates A Lan, a gay man who cruises Beijing's public toilets in search of homosexual sex, in Zhang Yuan's *East Palace, West Palace* (1996). Moving from the repressed cop to a clearly gay character in Stanley Kwan's *Lan Yu* (2001), Hu Jun brings another dimension to his role as SP Luk — SP Wong's rival and buddy. Having played closeted characters, Hu Jun brings that quality — i.e., that he has something to hide — to SP Luk. As noted earlier, Chen Daoming's association with the Emperor Qin from Zhang Yimou's *Hero* adds a similar weight to the character of Shen/Shadow in *Infernal Affairs III*. He seems to take on more than the role of gun runner/undercover cop and grow in stature as the only major male figure in the trilogy who survives without being confined to a wheelchair. Although he does end up with a limp and his future as a cross-border operative seems "shadowy," he does endure, like the Emperor Qin, to tie up the narrative if not all the loose ends of the crisis of the state.

Infernal Affairs brings this performance ensemble together to cover all the bases — i.e., Hong Kong, PRC, Taiwan, overseas Chinese, radio, television, Cantopop, rock, radio, art film, and indies. Moreover, this motley group manages to pull together and play off of each other's performances in order to tell a coherent story presented within a unified visual design. However, just as the performance styles vary throughout the trilogy, the "look" of the film and the operation of its narrative contain contradictions, and these tensions contribute to the construction of the trilogy as a global screen commodity.

6

Thieves and Pirates:
Beyond "Auteur" Cinema

As a commodity, *Infernal Affairs* floats within a global market. Gilles Deleuze notes that this floating culture has been colonized by clichés:

> They are these floating images, these anonymous clichés, which circulate in the external world, but which also penetrate each one of us and constitute his internal world, so that everyone possesses only psychic clichés by which he thinks and feels, is thought and is felt, being himself a cliché among the others in the world which surround him.[1]

Infernal Affairs self-consciously reflects on its use of clichés. At the climactic moment that Lau finds himself under Chan's gun in *Infernal Affairs I,* he remarks on the clichéd nature of their encounter by asking, "Do all undercover cops like rooftops?" Even phrases like "Sorry, I'm a cop" are repeated *ad nauseum.* From the repetition of clichés like "what goes around comes around" and "tomorrow is another day" to clichéd references to a popular cultural imagination of the world of cops and crooks, *Infernal Affairs* keeps its characters within this world of clichés.

As a form of mimicry, the cliché calls up a history of colonialism as it bridges the gap between Hollywood and Hong Kong films. "What goes around" in Hollywood, in fact, "comes around" in Hong Kong, and *Infernal Affairs* situates the clichés of the gangster genre within the specific circumstances of Hong Kong and its film culture. Stephen Teo notes the gangster genre has pushed Hong Kong cinema culture to the edge:

> ... in terms of their description of human behaviour in extremis, the thin line dividing enforcers of the law and criminals, together with the unwritten code that binds them together, gangster movies have constantly pushed Hong Kong cinema over the edge. They are rough, raw and jagged — often frighteningly so. A Hong Kong gangster movie can make viewers feel that civilization is indeed at risk and that Hong Kong is the last place on earth they would want to be.[2]

Although speaking of Wong Kar-wai's forays into the gangster genre, Ackbar Abbas's remarks also echo *Infernal Affairs'* slippage between the clichés of the genre and the self-conscious contemplation of the cinematic image:

> If the formulaic demands of the genre of the gangster film imply colonization and self-colonization by clichés, and if subverting the formulaic is not viable for a number of reasons (such as the need to get financial support to make films), there is still a third possibility: that of doing something else within the genre, of nudging it a little from its stable position and so provoking thought. This is postcoloniality not in the form of an argument; it takes the form of a new practice of the image.[3]

Infernal Affairs presents two types of film in one package. Director Andrew Lau, with his background as a cinematographer, contributes primarily to the visual design of the trilogy — its dramatic use of Hong Kong rooftops, its contrasting cool and warm colors, its organization of space on the streets and in office interiors. Co-director Alan Mak, as the co-screenwriter, takes on the task of storytelling and working with the ensemble cast on performance. *Infernal Affairs'* classic morality tale vies with its flamboyant visual style; however, both work together within a piece that is about both performance and image — looking the part as well as playing a role. The trilogy exists between cinema and television (coupled with other new technologies like computers and cell phones). The glamour, substance, depth, and complexity of cinema (from *The Godfather* to the Hong Kong New Wave) compete with the surface panache, spontaneity, and energy of television (from TVB to MTV).[4] Its fragmented style creates a balancing act between its art film roots and its express purpose to make money against the odds within an industry in crisis.[5]

Another layer of postmodern allegory clings to *Infernal Affairs*, and the trilogy not only alludes to other films and other media products, but it also tells the story of its own production within the context of Hong Kong and world cinema. Hong Kong cinema has always been positioned within a complex network of transnational relations, and *Infernal Affairs* displays the traces of this history. In fact, the underworld economy within the trilogy's narrative mirrors the political economy underpinning the Hong Kong cinema industry. Hong Kong productions have always been created by and catered to a transnational population from mainland China, Southeast Asia and other parts of the Chinese diaspora, and, after 1949, Taiwan.[6] Capital and talent flowed into and through Hong Kong, because of its colonial connections and borders, and ties to Shanghai, Bangkok, Saigon, Singapore, Kuala Lumpur, Honolulu, San Francisco, London, New York, and elsewhere run deep. Particularly during the Cold War, "left-wing" studios, with ties to production facilities and markets in the PRC, and "right-wing" studios, catering to markets in the ROC, competed for the Hong Kong and the overseas Chinese market. During the Cultural Revolution, the "left wing" studios were cut off from the Mainland, but Taiwan continued to ban films and filmmakers perceived to be sympathetic to Communism.

The end of martial law in Taiwan and the easing of cross-straits relations with the opening of the Mainland to Taiwan's business community have not eliminated the cinematic tug of war between the PRC and the ROC within the Hong Kong film industry. Although competition from Hollywood has intensified, Taiwan continues to be an important market, and the prestige of the Golden Horse Awards as well as box office receipts mean something to Hong Kong filmmakers like Lau and Mak.[7] The voice of Tsai Chin and the presence of Elva Hsiao nod to the continuing importance of Taiwan for Hong Kong filmmakers, and talent that frequently moves back and forth between Taiwan and Hong Kong, like Anthony Wong and Tony Leung, can only be a plus for a production like *Infernal Affairs*.

However, just as Yeung gets points with his PRC cohorts when he repatriates the Taiwanese gun runners, *Infernal Affairs* cannot turn its back on its relationship to the PRC as a source of talent, financing, and potential market. Since the opening of China to foreign investment and trade in the late 1970s, the Hong Kong film industry quickly revitalized its old ties across the border through traditionally "left-wing" studios as well as other players in joint-venture co-production initiatives. However, the relationship between the film industries in Hong Kong and the PRC has been rocky. With tight restrictions on the import of films into the PRC, even co-productions had difficulty finding an audience across the border. While Hong Kong films are considered "Chinese" in Taiwan and can compete on an equal footing with films made locally, Hong Kong films are imports in the PRC and, thus, subject to quotas and other restrictions. Under "one country, two systems," this has continued to be true after 1997. However, with the gradual implementation of CEPA (Closer Economic Partnership Agreement), this will eventually change. Even before its complete implementation, it made sense for Lau and Mak to work with the Tianjin Film Studios as a co-producer in *Infernal Affairs III*. They also draw in Mainland talent for *Infernal Affairs II* and *III*, so that Hu Jun and Chen Daoming become major players in the drama — and, perhaps, box-office draws across the border. Shen/Shadow/ Chen Daoming survives the trilogy as a symbol of Hong Kong cinema's closer links to the Mainland in the future.

Even though Thailand, as part of the Golden Triangle, is known for opium production and heroin trafficking, it still forms a major link in the narrative's imagination of Hong Kong's illegal cocaine trade. Although it may not make much sense in terms of drugs, it makes enormous sense in terms of the film industry.[8] With a history of overseas Chinese involvement in all aspects of society that spans centuries, Thailand has more recently emerged as an increasingly important site for film production and marketing. The government has seeded Bangkok's international film festival, and conditions for film production have improved exponentially as well. Filming in Bangkok not only nods to a traditionally important market for Hong Kong films within and beyond Thailand's substantial Chinese community, but also points to increased opportunities for cost-effective co-productions between Bangkok and Hong Kong. Sam, as well as Hong Kong filmmakers, take Bangkok as a second home, and filmmakers like Danny Pang, who edited all the *Infernal Affairs* films, have been very successful working between Thailand and Hong Kong. Drawing on Thai and Hong Kong talent, *The Eye* (2002), which Danny Pang made with his twin brother Oxide, with funds from Singapore's Raintree Productions, turned out to be a global success. In fact, *Infernal Affairs II* also drew on Raintree Productions for resources.

Although Hawaii proves to be a dead-end for *Infernal Affairs'* principals and only minor characters drift in from the United States as hired hands at the service of the triads, Hollywood — and America as a source of inspiration and potential market — insistently clings to the trilogy. Martin Scorsese's remake of *Infernal Affairs* as *The Departed* distributed by Warner Brothers[9] brings the ring of influence full circle. Although set within the world of the Irish mob in Boston, *The Departed* stars Italian (German) American Leonardo DiCaprio playing the Tony Leung role. Since his breakthrough feature *Mean Streets* (1973), Scorsese — along with directors such as Francis Ford Coppola, Michael Cimino, Abel Ferrara, Brian De Palma, and Quentin Tarantino — has been an Italian American filmmaker associated with the crime genre. More recently, another Italian American, David Chase (*né* De Cesare), has added a new dimension to screen portrayals of gangsters with his cable television series *The Sopranos* — drawing on directing talent like Mike Figgis who established himself on the big screen with films about corruption like *Internal Affairs* (1990). Many Italian American stars have been associated with these films and others featuring gangsters, including Robert De Niro, Al Pacino, John Travolta, and Nicolas Cage (*né* Nicholas Kim Coppola, Francis Ford Coppola's nephew). Moreover, several Italian American crime stories deal with undercover police in the Mafia and/or corruption within the police force; e.g., *Serpico* (1973), *Prince of the City* (1981), *Donnie Brasco* (1997).

The Godfather (1972), made during a time of national crisis at the height of American discontent with the war in Vietnam, merges a sense of ethnic alienation from the promise of the American dream with a more general malaise surrounding the excesses of the military-industrial establishment.[10] Although the cinematic gangster of Prohibition and the Depression had his undeniable appeal, the gangster of the New American Cinema, beginning in the 1970s, embodied a moral ambiguity compounded by ethnic otherness, a crisis in patriarchal authority, and the rapidly changing mores of a nation under siege from within. Through the millennium, the new American gangster continues to represent a society in conflict embroiled in the excesses of capitalism and searching for spiritual relief everywhere from established religion to psychiatry.

In fact, the Hong Kong and American screen gangster share a similar social milieu marked by rapid change, mercurial identities, and economic panic. Several Hong Kong filmmakers have borrowed liberally from Hollywood Italian characterizations of the gangster (e.g., Brian De Palma's *The Untouchables*, 1987, on Al Capone, becomes the basis for Kirk Wong's *Gunmen* — 1988, with cinematography by Andrew Lau — on Shanghai triads).[11] Italian American filmmakers have been attracted to Hong Kong triads as a parallel to their own interest in the Italian mafia. As occult criminal organizations, the mafia and the triads have certain historical characteristics in common. Within Italy and China, they have their roots in discontent with what was perceived to be illegitimate government authority, and they offered protection against other even more violent forces in the society at the time by claiming patriotic motives. The mafia and triads often crossed the thin line between protection in a lawless society and extortion adding to social chaos.

In the "new world" of the United States, colonial Hong Kong, or elsewhere, Italian and Chinese émigrés needed protection from exploitation based on racism and prejudice, and the mafia and triads filled a void for those excluded from the mainstream culture and its criminal justice system. As newcomers became more acclimated to their adopted countries, triads and the mafia needed other sources of income. Occult and outside the law, they gravitated to vice — liquor, gambling, prostitution, narcotics — while maintaining a foothold in the related areas of loan sharking and extortion while moving into non-criminal activities; e.g., entertainment, real estate, etc. Throughout their histories, the mafia and triads have had an ambivalent relationship to their host societies. There has been open celebration of triad support for the

KMT and its activities; the Mafia fought fascism in Sicily, pushed an election in favor of an underdog candidate for president in the United States, etc. However, police and other branches of the government in Hong Kong, Europe, and the United States have also openly gone to war against secret societies.

Because of this historical ambivalence, the Italian and Chinese underworlds provide a meeting ground for filmmakers interested in the drama of economic inequality, the dark side of capitalism, the addictions of consumerism, alienation from the "nation," the crisis in government authority, and identity crises resulting from an increasingly complex technological society to changing notions of gender, sexuality, and ethnicity. Hong Kong on the cusp of influences from the PRC, Taiwan, Britain, and the US, but separate from them all, and Italian America with just enough ethnic, cultural, historical, and religious difference to be separate from the Anglo-American mainstream find themselves positioned similarly to use the gangster as an emblem of a more general social discontent.

Therefore, Hong Kong and Italian American filmmakers working in the gangster genre have quite a bit in common and a mutual interest in each other's output should be expected. Michael Cimino (*Year of the Dragon*, 1985) and Abel Ferrara (*China Girl*, 1987) have taken up the subject of the relationship between the Italian mafia and the Chinese triads in New York City. As well as making *The Departed* based on *Infernal Affairs*, Scorsese also found inspiration in Chinese history for his film on the Dalai Lama *Kundun* (1997). When Quentin Tarantino made *Reservoir Dogs* (1992), he turned to Hong Kong for inspiration and remade Ringo Lam's *City on Fire* (1987). Both films are about an undercover cop who infiltrates a gang. The thin line between cop and crook as well as the conflicted morality of betraying trust within a group of thieves feed into a slew of other films including *Infernal Affairs*. John Woo has turned this theme into a key element of much of his oeuvre, including *A Better Tomorrow* (1986), *The Killer* (1989), *Hard Boiled* (1992), and *Face/Off* (1997). Coming full circle, Woo cast John Travolta (from Tarantino's *Pulp Fiction*) and Nicolas Cage (a member of the Coppola clan) in *Face/Off* as cop and crook who switch identities — the main inspiration for the script of *Infernal Affairs*.[12]

Earlier, this profound ambivalence surrounding the depiction of the triads came to the surface in Andrew Lau's successful series *Young and Dangerous* (1996–2000), based on a popular comic book and scripted by Manfred Wong.[13] Controversial for supposedly glamorizing the triads by giving them a youthful, "hip" new image,[14] the series appeared simultaneously with a spike in triad activity within the film industry as well as a triad push to recruit new members from the public schools because of the manpower shortage occasioned by Hong Kong's vibrant economy in the late 1980s and 1990s that made triad involvement less attractive.

Several films made in the 1990s paid tribute to triad kingpins. Publicity surrounding triad infiltration into the film industry peaked during 1992 when Anita Mui became embroiled in two gangland assassinations (of Wong Long-wai and Andely "Tiger" Chan) and film producer/former drug smuggler Jim Choi was gunned down the same year.[15] Fredric Dannen even quotes Wong Kar-wai as saying, "It's better to deal with a godfather than an accountant."[16]

In many ways, *Infernal Affairs* plays as a continuation of Andrew Lau's popular *Young and Dangerous*. When Sam talks about moving out from Tuen Mun as he rallies his young recruits to join the ranks of the police, he seems to address the young hoods from the earlier series with the promise of fresh faces, trendy styles, and hip characterization to reinvigorate Hong Kong popular notions of the triad genre.[17] Running parallel to the year leading up to the handover and concluding at the millennium, the series covered many of the themes taken up by the *Infernal Affairs* trilogy, including the impact of the handover on the triad economy, the increasing importance of the PRC as a factor, global ties with Taiwan, Japan, and Thailand as hedges against the local Hong Kong situation, gang warfare linked to capitalist expansion, and the crisis in traditional notions of Chinese patriarchy and masculinity as the young triads come of age in a different world from their predecessors. Just as Ringo Lam's *School on Fire* (1988), Wilson Yip's *Mongkok Story* (1996), and Fruit Chan's independently produced *Made in Hong Kong* (1997) present a bleak picture of young hoods, *Infernal Affairs* takes *Young and Dangerous* to its logical conclusion by showing the downfall of the triads.

The Author as Brand Name

One of the primary ways *Infernal Affairs* rests on the repression of Hong Kong New Wave cinema as a basis for its own re-imagination of the Hong Kong film as a transnational product involves its references to and denial of the New Wave auteur. The "auteur" functions less as an "author" and more as a "brand" with a "name" as the guarantee of a specific market niche. Part of the rise of the co-directed, international blockbuster (e.g., films by the Cohen Brothers, the Wachowski Brothers, Johnnie To/Wai Ka-fai), *Infernal Affairs* moves beyond the personal film and the obsessions of a single auteur into a creative environment, which revolves around anti-individualism and eclecticism.[18]

However, the trilogy is also in constant conversation with its New Wave antecedents — particularly the oeuvre of Wong Kar-wai (Andrew Lau's former collaborator) and his stylistic flourishes, interest in time, obsession with popular culture, allegorical references, etc. Like other postmodern films, *Infernal Affairs* dissolves the borders between popular and high culture, and it turns its allusive nature from a reliance on esoteric references to a common vocabulary based on comic books, Hollywood film, and pulp fiction. To this, it adds a high degree of self-consciousness regarding its own creation.[19]

In this regard, it joins a long tradition of gangster films with self-reflexive stylistics; e.g., Jean-Luc Godard's *Breathless* (1959) and other gangster meditations from the French New Wave (e.g., Jean-Pierre Melville's *Le Samourai*, 1967), Oshima Nagisa's *Diary of a Shinjuku Thief* (1968), etc. Other films feature the Japanese New Wave's obsession with yakuza gangs, the PRC's Sixth Generation's preoccupation with petty hoods, Taiwan's New Cinema's interest in the triads, and, of course, Hong Kong New Wave's forays into the gangster genre in Wong Kar-wai's films.

Filmmakers have a profound connection to the world of the gangster in which image is everything, competition rife, and survival means scoring the next deal to continue operating. Godard made that perfectly clear in his oeuvre, and it sticks to *Infernal Affairs*. The filmmakers must go through the same elaborate negotiations as the gangster to put their package together, produce it, distribute it, and make a profit. Chan on the cell phone or Keung boasting of the market in European or American stolen cars "re-exported" in Hong Kong for the Mainland market parallels the "re-export" of pirated DVDs of Hollywood films (or Hong Kong versions of Hollywood commercial fare) that flow through Hong Kong as a transshipment point on their way to the PRC.[20] Given the PRC's limited legal distribution of foreign films, the demand for pirated DVDs and VCDs runs high,[21] and Hong Kong triads happily take a cut of the action. However, in an industry plagued by the infiltration of actual gangsters and illegal competition from video pirates, the filmmakers also have a profound identification with the forces of law and order to protect their business interests. Like Chan and Lau, filmmakers fall between the cracks that divide cops and crooks. Drawing directly on the work of other filmmakers to compete with an aggressive Hollywood product, they are, in turn, harassed by the illegal trade in their creative property.

The copy, in fact, troubles the waters of an industry in crisis while also fueling its creative energy. In *One-Way Street*, Walter

Benjamin puts his finger on the power of the copy by referring to the traditional Chinese practice of copying books:

> The power of the country road is different when one is walking along it from when one is flying over it by airplane. In the same way, the power of a text is different when it is read from when it is copied out. The airplane passenger sees only how the road pushes through the landscape, how it unfolds according to the same laws as the terrain surrounding it. Only he who walks the road on foot learns of the power it commands, and of how, from the very scenery that for the flier is only the unfurled plain, it calls forth distances, belvederes, clearings, prospects at each of its turns like a commander deploying soldiers at a front. Only the copied text commands the soul of him who is occupied with it, whereas the mere reader never discovers the new aspects of his inner self that are opened by the text, that road cut through the interior jungle forever closing behind it: because the reader follows the movement of this mind in the free flight of daydreaming, whereas the copier submits it to command. The Chinese practice of copying books was thus an incomparable guarantee of literary culture, and the transcript a key to China's enigmas.[22]

As Benjamin notes, the issue may rest with the perspective taken toward art — from the point of view of a leisurely stroll or the flight of a speeding airplane. Whether this provides a key to either "China's enigmas" or *Infernal Affairs* remains moot. However, the copy may offer a "guarantee" of Hong Kong's cinematic culture.

It seems appropriate, ultimately, that the filmmakers allegorize their role as creative observers in the figure of Lau's wife Mary (Sammi Cheng, who has made a career as a film comedienne and pop singer). In *Infernal Affairs I*, Mary scrutinizes the enigmatic Lau, imagines him with multiple hidden personalities, and fails to determine whether he's a "good guy" or a "bad guy." Drunk in *Infernal Affairs II* (played by Chiu Chung-yue), Mary seems confused about her own identity and has trouble even spelling her name. In *Infernal Affairs III*, Mary finally walks away from Lau. However, Lau continues to fascinate as an image — the "face" of Hong Kong for the world — and Andrew Lau and Alan Mak do not walk away from his star presence but allow him to fill the screen in close-up as the final image of the film — a gesture of faith in Hong Kong, its film industry, and the glamour of its constructed identity as "Asia's world city."

As the trilogy ends, coincidence draws a fine line between chance and fate. The directors' fortuitous use of "Forgotten Times" provides a key to understanding the workings of karma in the film. Chan and Lau share a common destiny — each trapped in a hell, at least partially of his own making, and fated to lose everything — including his identity. Although Chan has his upright police persona restored on his tombstone at the end of the first *Infernal Affairs*, it comes too late for the character to realize his dream of coming out from undercover. Lau ends up taking on Chan's identity as he sinks into madness, tapping out his own Morse code message to himself near the end of *Infernal Affairs III*. Both are lost to themselves.

However, a contradiction exists between *Infernal Affairs'* vision of the crisis of masculinity, global capitalism, and government legitimacy and its success as a transnational commercial product. The Hong Kong genre film has been "reincarnated" in the context of the global film market. Like *Crouching Tiger Hidden Dragon* and *Hero*, *Infernal Affairs* provides a fantasy that can cross borders and find new life for producers in search of reliable profits. Andrew Lau, for example, has been snatched up by Hollywood to direct *The Flock*, starring Richard Gere as a federal officer.[23] Again, coming full circle, the villain of *Internal Affairs* (1990) works with the director of *Infernal Affairs*.

Situated somewhere between pessimism and consumer exuberance, *Infernal Affairs* fits within the global postmodern crystallized in postcolonial Hong Kong described by Evans Chan as:

> ... moving from the old century into the new one, postmodernism seems still fairly young and post-colonial Hong Kong is a mere infant. But this age does induce profound pessimism. Thoughts, politics, and history are all being commodified and processed by the all-embracing media in the periodic artificial excitement of fashion and consumerism.[24]

Within postmodernity, the question of identity — national, ethnic, class, and sexual — speaks to a global crisis, and the fate of two moles in Hong Kong captivates viewers whose "forgotten times" may have nothing to do with Greater China but everything to do with the decay of the patriarchy, transnational capitalism, and the crisis of the nation-state. As generic cycles echo the karmic cycles of Buddhism, "continuous hell" metamorphoses into the continuous dramatic, visual, and thematic revival of Hong Kong commercial cinema through the turn of the New Wave art house wheel of cinematic fate.

Appendix 1

Plot Summaries

Infernal Affairs

The first film begins with the initiation of Lau Kin-ming (Edison Chen) into the triads by his immediate boss Sam (Eric Tsang). Sam has assigned the new triad recruits to a deep cover infiltration of the Hong Kong police force, and Lau next appears as a police cadet. Superintendent Wong (Anthony Wong Chau-sang) and Academy Principal Yip (Fung Hui-kam) recruit Chan Wing-yan (Shawn Yue), another cadet in the academy, to go undercover as a mole within the triads. Arrested, Chan transforms from Shawn Yue into Tony Leung Chiu-wai, who plays the older incarnation of the character. Promoted in the force, Lau changes from Edison Chen to Andy Lau, who plays the older Lau Kin-ming.

Chan and Lau meet in a stereo store, where Chan pretends to be the proprietor when Lau comes in to purchase some equipment. They sit and listen to Tsai Chin's "Forgotten Times" in order to test the equipment, and Lau is sold on the system. Lau leaves, the real owner arrives, and Chan rushes out to attend the funeral of his police academy mentor SP Yip. SP Wong now becomes the only officer in the force who knows Chan's true identity. Chan has worked for Sam for three years (and has been undercover for ten); however, he still does not enjoy the unquestioned trust of his underworld boss. Wong orders Chan to see a psychiatrist to help him deal with his frequent violent outbursts in order to stay out of jail.

Parallel to Sam's preparations for a drug deal with his Thai contacts, SP Wong plots a bust to foil Sam's plans. However, the work of each mole cancels the other out, and Sam and Wong both fail. At home, Lau begins to organize his new apartment with his bride, Mary (Sammi Cheng), when Sam calls to give him the task of ferreting out the mole in the gangs. Mary, a writer, alludes to using Lau as her inspiration for a story about a man with multiple personalities — "a good guy who has done bad things." Picking up on the idea of psychiatric disorders, *Infernal Affairs* cuts to Chan visiting his psychiatrist, Dr. Lee Sum-yee (Kelly Chen).

Impressed by his settling down to marry his girlfriend Mary, Lau's superiors give him a promotion and move him to Internal Affairs with the mission of finding Sam's mole within the force. In order to find the police mole for Sam, Lau has devised a scheme in which Sam's underlings fill out forms that he will match against police files. Chan's plan to find the mole in the force involves following Sam to the meeting in which these forms will be passed along to the other mole. Wong lets slip that he plans to have Sam followed until he leads him to the mole, and Lau takes up this same strategy to flush out the undercover cop. Lau has Wong followed, and he pinpoints a meeting between Wong and Chan, calls it in, and the gangsters make a plan to intercept the cops at their office building rendezvous. Chan gets a call that the mole has been located, and the cops move in on the same location. Wong does not slip by the gangsters and is killed, and Chan needs to be rescued by another gangster Keung (Chapman To). Keung has been shot, and he eventually dies in Chan's arms.

Rummaging through Wong's effects, Lau discovers the cell phone he used to communicate with the mole, and Lau uses the Morse code signal to get Chan to make contact with him. Still ignorant of Lau's true identity, Chan agrees to meet his new handler, and Lau involves him in a plot that leads to Sam's death. Back at the police station, Lau's fellow officers applaud him for killing Sam. Chan discovers the file envelope that held the triad profiles for Sam, and he realizes Lau is the mole. When Lau returns to find Chan has left, he also understands that Chan knows about his true identity, and, in retaliation, Lau returns to the computer in order to wipe out all evidence of Chan's undercover status.

Chan seeks sanctuary from Dr. Lee, and reminds her to prove his undercover identity if something should happen to him. Meanwhile, Mary plays a recording of Lau that Sam had made — his "insurance" policy in case Lau ever turned on him — and Mary now knows Lau is Sam's mole. Chan and Lau meet on a rooftop, and Chan handcuffs Lau planning on taking him in. However, one of Lau's operatives, Billy, arrives on the scene and pulls a gun on Chan. Holding guns on each other, Chan and Billy move with Lau to the elevator. As the doors open, Billy kills Chan, gives the gun to Lau, and reveals the fact that he too is one of Sam's moles. He has destroyed the incriminating tape with Sam and Lau's voices on it, and he pledges loyalty to his new triad boss Lau. They get into the elevator, a gunshot is heard, and Lau emerges alone holding his badge up for the uniformed cops on the scene, proclaiming he's "a cop." Dr. Lee finds confirmation in Yip's files that Chan, indeed, was an undercover cop, and Lau officiates at the funeral.

Infernal Affairs II

Infernal Affairs II begins in 1991. Wong talks about his first arrest. He soliloquizes about the death of his partner at the hands of a triad working for the Ngai family. He tells this story to one of Ngai's minions, Sam, in the hope of enlisting him in a plan to eliminate Ngai. Loyal to the Ngai family, Sam declines Wong's invitation and gets into a car with his wife Mary (Carina Lau) to leave the station. Young Lau (Edison Chen) takes the contract and shoots Ngai Kwun. He reports back to Mary who ordered the hit — kept secret from Sam.

Chan Wing-yan (Shawn Yue) catches Keung attempting to steal a young woman's car. Superintendent Luk (Hu Jun) drives up to take over the arrest, and Luk reminds Chan that he should not be overly zealous as a police cadet. Luk, Yip, and Chan have a formal dinner in a restaurant and talk about the future of the police force after 1997. After dinner, a mysterious car pulls in front of them, and Ngai Wing-hau (Francis Ng), the son of murdered triad boss Ngai Kwun, steps out to tell Chan, his half-brother, about their father's death.

At a hot pot restaurant, four of Kwun's associates meet to discuss the implications of his assassination. The "Big Four" — Negro, Ching, Wah, and Gandhi — decide that, with the patriarch's death, the clan will not be able to hold on to its underworld empire, and they plan to break away from the Ngai family. SP Wong and SP Luk stand by for a gang war. However, Ngai Wing-hau is a step ahead, and he sends Sam in to mediate as he blackmails and cajoles each of the four mutineers into remaining subordinates within the Ngai organization.

Because of his blood tie to the Ngai clan, Chan must leave the police academy, and SP Wong steps in to recruit Chan as an undercover agent. Chan says that he relishes the opportunity to arrest his half-brother himself, and Chan begins his life undercover as an inmate in prison.

By 1995 when the action resumes, Lau has ensconced himself within the police department. Chan also begins to earn the trust of his half-brother who invites him to take a more active role in the family business. With 1997 approaching, Ngai devises a plan to turn over his business interests to Negro, Ching, Wah, and Gandhi, when he emigrates. However, he confides in Sam that he actually plans to go into business with a Thai gang involved in cocaine smuggling. Sam and Keung set out for Bangkok. Mary phones to warn Sam that he is in danger, but she fails to convince him to cancel his trip. She meets with SP Wong in a hotel room, and they try to decide what to do about Ngai, since they had conspired to kill his father.

Wong and Luk devise an operation to catch Ngai making a deal with two Americans. They arrest him as he makes an exchange, and they bring him into the police station. Although Sam, after finally accepting Mary's warning, escapes the assassination attempt in Bangkok, the other four gangsters meet grizzly ends. During the course of Ngai's interrogation, the contents of the briefcase become known. The Americans were private detectives who uncovered Wong's conspiracy with Mary to assassinate Kwun, and Ngai has captured this on tape in order to bring Wong's involvement to the authorities. Privy to the plot, Lau manages to stop the attempt on Mary's life and take her to a secluded location in Hong Kong's New Territories.

In retaliation, gangsters drive by to shoot Ngai, and Chan saves his life by taking a bullet in the shoulder. Luk visits Wong to tell him that the police department will support him, even though he conspired to murder Kwun. They agree to go in together. However, when Luk starts Wong's car to drive to the station, the car explodes, killing Luk. Still in Bangkok, Sam tries to negotiate with one of his Thai attackers for safe passage out of the country, but he ends up getting shot in the chest instead. When Mary suspects something is seriously wrong, she tries to leave for Bangkok, but Lau tries to stop her and sexually assaults her. Mary fights off Lau's sexual advances and escapes. Lau secretly arranges her death and watches as she is killed at the airport.

Time shifts to 1997. Wong has his eleventh hearing on his involvement with Kwun's death and Lau comes up for promotion within the force. Lau gets his promotion, and Wong is exonerated and can resume his duties. Sam has been located in Thailand, and Wong goes to convince him to come back to Hong Kong and testify against Ngai. Meanwhile, Ngai has plans to take advantage of the handover to move away from the rackets and win a seat in the Hong Kong legislature. However, during a meeting with higher-ups from the People's Republic, Wong steps in and arrests Ngai, thwarting his plans for a political career. Worried about Sam's plan to testify against him, Ngai sends his immediate family to Hawaii and another member of the family to Thailand in order to put pressure on Sam by threatening his new wife and child.

Sam, with Lau's help, escapes from police custody to meet Ngai. Sam has located Ngai's family in Hawaii, and he also has his Thai underlings in control of his own interests in Bangkok. Although Ngai has a gun to Sam's head, Sam has Ngai checkmated. When the police arrive, they put a bullet through Ngai's forehead, and Sam goes free. As he dies in Chan's arms, a final blow comes when Ngai discovers that Chan wears a wire, indicating he has been a mole in the gang.

During the handover, Wong, Lau, and the other police replace their colonial insignia with the new crest of the police force under the HKSAR administration. Sam takes a moment to reflect on Mary's passing as fireworks light up Hong Kong harbor, before he goes off to join the revelers on July 1, 1997. Keung takes Chan under his wing after Ngai's death, and Lau returns to his duties at the police station. A young woman comes in drunk, and Lau takes the statement from Mary (Chiu Chung-yue who plays the younger version of Sammi Cheng's character), clearly smitten with the new Mary in front of him.

Infernal Affairs III

Infernal Affairs III opens with Keung telling Chan (Tony Leung) to stop his rampage in a massage parlor. Keung, who did not get the service he expected at the brothel, called in Chan to enforce his authority. The film shifts to events after Chan's death and picks up on Lau's hearing. However, since the surveillance camera in the elevator had been disabled and cannot be used to corroborate Lau's story, he ends up with a temporary post in Administration. Although things look bright at the police force, Lau begins to experience a mental breakdown.

SP Yeung (Leon Lai), from the Security Unit, appears on the scene. After one mole commits suicide in Yeung's office, Lau begins to keep an eye on Yeung as a threat. If Yeung is also a mole, he could be trying to eliminate the others as threats to the security of his own cover. If a loyal cop, he threatens Lau with exposure. In any case, Lau becomes obsessed with Yeung and makes elaborate provisions to keep him under constant surveillance. Lau uncovers a connection between Yeung and Shen (Chen Daoming), an arms dealer from the PRC and one of Sam's former business partners.

Lau also wants to get at Dr. Lee's computer files on Chan. Lau has set up Lee's office to look as if it has been burglarized, and he tricks Lee into revealing the password for her computer so he can gain access. Lau learns that Chan has sent a tape to Dr. Lee. Lee claims not to have listened to the tape, so Lau stages a car accident as a pretext to neutralize the incriminating tape.

The film moves between events in 2003 and 2002. Using intelligence from Chan, Wong plans to move in on the deal between Shen and Sam. However, Yeung steps in, and, after bringing in Internal Affairs, stops Wong's planned sting operation. Sam decides to pull out of the operation and leaves Chan to his own devices in dealing with Shen and the aborted arms deal. Keung pleads for Chan, but Sam simply drives away.

In 2003, Lau executes an elaborate plot to drug the officers in the Security Unit and rob Yeung's office safe. Successful, Lau parades the cassette he pilfered from Yeung's safe in the station and sets out to confront Yeung. Shen also appears in the office. The film cuts back to the arms deal of the year before. With the deal gone sour, Shen goes after Chan and wounds him in the arm (explaining the cast he wears in *Infernal Affairs I*). Chan shoots Shen in the leg. He manages to capture Chan and put a gun to his head. Yeung arrives on the scene and tells Shen he is welcome to kill Chan and save him the hassle of an arrest. However, Shen has come to the realization that Chan is not really working for Sam, and they all reveal that, indeed, they are cops; i.e., Shen undercover from the PRC, Chan undercover for OCTB (Organized Crime and Triad Bureau), and Yeung from the Security Unit.

The film returns to 2003, and Lau plays a recording of a conversation he has with Sam — proving he is the mole. However, in his delirium, he does not identify with his own voice and claims the conversation takes place between Yeung and Sam. Lau shoots Yeung through the forehead, and Shen wings Lau. Lau holds a gun to his own jaw and fires in a suicide attempt which sends him to the hospital. Lau's wife Mary visits him in the sanitarium, where he is confined to a wheelchair. The concluding scene of the trilogy goes back to Chan's meeting with Lau at the stereo store, and the third film ends with Lau asking to try out the system as Tsai Chin sings "Forgotten Times."

Appendix 2

Interview with
Andrew Lau and Alan Mak

Conducted on November 3, 2004, at Base Production Ltd., by Gina Marchetti and Amy Lee for *Hong Kong CineMagic* with the assistance of Thomas Podvin

Reprinted from *Hong Kong CineMagic*, http://www.hkcinemagic.com/en/page.asp?aid=59&page=0

On *Infernal Affairs*

How did Infernal Affairs *first get off the ground?*

Alan Mak/AM: Around 1998, I saw *Face/Off* (John Woo, 1997), and I really liked that movie. For John Woo, it is quite difficult to make a movie in Hollywood in his own style. Because Hollywood is based on a producer system, it is difficult for a director to express himself using his own style of filmmaking. In this case, John Woo had the right to the final cut, and it turned out very well. The surgery about changing the face and body, however, was really not believable. So, with that movie as inspiration, I began to start to think about a story in which two people swap identities. *Infernal Affairs* really started from there. In Hong Kong, there are so many movies about undercover cops, but we didn't have any about a triad member infiltrating the police. Actually, I think it must happen, so *Infernal Affairs* came out of that idea. Actually, I think all the filmmakers in Hong Kong are influenced by John Woo.

Did you conceive of Infernal Affairs *primarily as a police story or as an action film?*

AM: From the beginning, we were being pressured to put more action in the film. During the marketing of the film, for example, I was asked if I could put more action scenes in it. So, I asked them how much more money the film would make if I put in more action, but they couldn't answer my question. From the beginning, I did want to put another three to four minutes more into the action scenes, but Andrew would not consider it, because he thought the drama is really more attractive to the audience.

People always ask how you can find Tony Leung and Andy Lau to act in this movie. It's not common to see the two of them in the same film. Because Hong Kong movies were going through a bad time, they both wanted to find a good project so that they could cooperate and make a good film. They read the script, and they were attracted to the idea. Having a script before a project comes together is not common in Hong Kong. In this case, it helped quite a bit to have a strong script.

How did you come up with the look of the film and the visual effects?

Andrew Lau/AL: When I direct a script, because of my background as a cinematographer, the look of the film becomes essential. When I worked on *City on Fire* (Ringo Lam, 1987), the look of the film — lighting, dark images, camera movement — was very different — not the normal style for Hong Kong. I used a lot of green and blue in the color palette — using natural lighting without correction to give it that very distinctive look.

For *Infernal Affairs*, I worked very closely with Christopher Doyle who spent lots of time in the film laboratory working on the color — getting the "color timing" right — so that the colors would look the way I had wanted them to look. I wanted to design all the lighting, but I didn't want to have to fiddle with the lights a lot on location. I worked with the art directors on the lighting. For example, at the police station, we wanted to use fluorescent light. I controlled the on-location lighting design, but I still needed to work on the look of the film in post-production.

On location, we were so busy that I wanted to avoid the problem of adjusting the lights, so Christopher Doyle had a lot to do at the lab. He's good at lab work. He's patient, and I'm not patient with the lab. A lot of people asked why I would hire Christopher Doyle, since I'm an accomplished cinematographer, but he really helped with the post-production to create the look I wanted for *Infernal Affairs*. I trusted him to do it.

Could you talk about the soundtrack and how you chose the music for Infernal Affairs*?*

AL: It was easy to choose the Taiwanese pop music (Tsai Chin's "The Forgotten Times"), because we used that CD to test the sound system. The location scout always used that song to test the equipment. The song is really good, too.

Did you anticipate the success of Infernal Affairs *at the time you were making it? Did you know you were going to save the Hong Kong film industry with this film?*

AL: Of course not ... . That was a hard moment — a horrible time in Hong Kong. Box-office figures were so low. Before *Infernal Affairs*, I set up this company (Base Production Ltd.), and people thought I would lose money. A lot of people were talking about the Hong Kong film industry as a "sunset industry." People thought I had a lot of guts to set up a new company, and asked why. Why not? I only know movies, so what else can I do? We have to keep on going and make movies.

Even in the best of times, it's hard to knock on doors, find a producer and find investors. Media Asia liked the idea, and I talked to the executive producer there who understood it was a "high concept" film. He tried to push up the budget for us. I tried to do a calculation to determine how much I needed for the film. Even with the calculation, the deal was loose.

Even with 20 million Hong Kong dollars in box office, we would still lose money. Totally, the budget was 50 million Hong Kong dollars. The actors were one-third of the budget. At that time, the investors expected the budget to be 50/50 — cast and production costs — but I wanted more for the production costs to get the look I wanted for the film.

With that budget, I was able to use a full orchestra for the score. This was the first time in Hong Kong film history that a full orchestra was used for a film score. Before this, a synthesizer was used, but, this time, we used a real orchestra. A lot of the budget went into creating the quality you see on screen in the sets, the sound, and all the details — for example, a car we used for only one shot cost 20 thousand. We wanted to do something that was a good quality film.

Background as Filmmakers

Alan, could you talk about the flashbacks in X-Mas Rave Fever *(1999)?*

AM: It's a simple story. From the beginning, the producer at Golden Harvest wanted me to make a movie about a rave party in Hong Kong in the 1990s. I had not been to one, so I did some research on the topic for about three months. The producer said you cannot talk about drugs, sex, or any of the most interesting parts of the rave parties. So, I decided that I wanted to do a movie that had a distinctive narrative structure about a man who goes to a rave party, gets drunk, picks up a girl, forgets about her, and then tries to find out who the girl is. In the end, the girl is a man. It's just a simple story — organized in three parts — based on a structural premise that had not been used in Hong Kong film before this. It's a small movie, but I really like it.

Could you talk about the music in X-Mas Rave Fever*? Why did you choose Mark Lui and the OnLine band to write the score?*

AM: It is part of the contract. Because I needed Mark Lui as one of the actors and there wasn't enough money for him, we also contracted him to do the music.

Andrew, you've worked as a director, producer, and cinematographer. Which job do you prefer?

AL: I've worked as a cinematographer on so many films — *City on Fire*, *As Tears Go By*, *Young and Dangerous* — and so many others. Of course, I like directing, so I can be in control of the cinematography, the acting, etc. In Hong Kong, normally the actors have a lot of control, but I need to fully control everything. When I was a cameraman, I was very upset sometimes because I could not control everything. Even when you shoot a shot you don't like, the director can say it's okay, and it will end up in the film. So that's why I want to be the director.

When you directed the first installment of Young and Dangerous, *did you envision it would become a series?*

AL: No, of course not. When I did the first one, I thought of it as self-contained. After the box-office returns came in, we began to think of a series. At first, I didn't want to shoot this movie. I didn't want to make a movie involving the triads. One day, I was given a hot comic book and told to shoot the movie. I didn't like it, and I didn't want to do it. It had a lot of violence. After one or two weeks work, I began to turn it into another kind of movie. That's why I like the title *Young and Dangerous*. This movie gave me the opportunity to work with a group of up and coming actors — who weren't expensive — and make a movie for young people. I just took the background and some characters from the comic book, and Wong Jing allowed me to do something different. We shot it quickly, and, as we were finishing, I began to think of the second one, because we had so much material left. Then, we decided to do another one, but we still had to wait for the first one to be released. In fact, we had trouble getting the first one released because it had no stars and it seemed like just another triad movie. The distributors were old-fashioned and they didn't understand the youth culture in the film. The film is for young people — they didn't understand the costumes, hair styles, etc. They didn't know how to judge the film. Later on, we had a two-week period, but we didn't have a firm booking. We did, however, have the midnight screening slot, and word of mouth spread very quickly. Then, we were asked to shoot part two as fast as we could.

Alan, let me ask you about a film you did in Thailand, A War Named Desire *(2000). What was it like working in Thailand?*

AM: I like shooting movies in Thailand very much because the government is so cooperative there. The police help you to close the roads for shooting. The industry people are well trained, too, since they have supported a lot of Hollywood films — particularly war movies.

AL: Shooting in Thailand is easy. The costs in Thailand are reasonable, and the people are very open.

Andrew, could you tell us about your relationship with Wong Jing and Manfred Wong?

AL: I need more than two days to answer that question — we have such a long history together. Wong Jing was really my master when I was an assistant cameraman. We met a long time ago in 1981 when I was just a young kid. I worked with him. Later, when he left Shaw Brothers and went on to shoot so many successful movies, I also continued my career as a cameraman. We wanted to work together, but we never were able to be matched up on a project. In 1992, I joined his company (Wong Jing's Workshop) as a director. I shot several films which were not too successful, but also not too bad.

   In 1995, I shot *The Temple Street Story* (a.k.a. *The Mean Street Story*). At that time, Manfred Wong was a DJ on the radio, and he would review movies. He was a scriptwriter, but he had this late-night radio program as well to talk about movies. He said *The Temple Street Story* was a bad movie. Some people recorded Manfred's review and gave the tape to me. The promotion company told me this big mouth said your movie was no good. I thought, if I ever meet this guy ... So, I mentioned this all to Wong Jing. Wong Jing and Manfred Wong know each other well because they are around the same age. Wong Jing said, "Really?" I said, "Yes." So, Wong Jing picked up the phone, and he called Manfred and invited him to "yam cha" (drink tea). This was not what I wanted — I wanted Wong Jing to do something about Manfred. Wong Jing organized a meeting with Manfred and me. Wong Jing suggested that all three of us form a new company. So, we became friends because of Wong Jing.

At that time, we really started fresh — started a new life. The first movie for the new company was *Young and Dangerous* (1996). So, at that time, we became good friends, and we began to make lots of movies together. Even today, we are still good friends.

On the *Infernal Affairs* series

When did you get the idea for the second and third parts of Infernal Affairs?

AM: Andrew said let's see what happens. Before *Infernal Affairs* was released, Andrew was in Beijing shooting another movie. We were so worried because it was just 10 days before the film was scheduled to be released. Around the same time, another undercover movie came out, and it was a huge flop. Only about 100 viewers went to see that film. We weren't thinking of saving the industry when the film came out — just trying to do okay with it.

How did you go on with the story after the end of Infernal Affairs? *Was it a challenge to make parts two and three?*

AM: It was really difficult. Because when we wanted to shoot *Infernal Affairs III*, the investors wanted the same cast. I couldn't create a brother for Tony Leung and have him come back for revenge. It's too much like *A Better Tomorrow II* or something like that. So, we chose a way to tell the story in two different time periods. We used the character of Kelly Chen (Dr. Lee) to cross-over from the past into the future.

AL: Yes, that was quite difficult to match the action from the first with the third film and cross-over in a convincing way. We couldn't think of any better way to do it. Part II was easier. Part III was very challenging. We have a lot of fans with expectations, and we have to appease the audience in Hong Kong as well as mainland China. We need to strike a balance between the fans' desires and telling the story.

AM: It's also a big challenge for the audience. They aren't used to watching a commercial movie structured that way.

Was it difficult to get all the talent involved to work together?

AM: It wasn't difficult because of Andrew ...

AL: I'm the "Big Brother" (da ge/dai go). Andy, Tony, Anthony, Eric, we all worked together when I was young. So, I've known a lot of these famous actors for many years. Andy and Tony looked at the script, and I asked which character each wanted to do. At that moment, they knew which character they wanted. Their choices ended up being suitable. I wasn't sure about the chemistry, and I wanted to change, but it really turned out right.

Notes

Chapter 1   Introduction: The New Wave and the Generic Abyss

1. Lisa Odham Stokes and Michael Hoover, *City on Fire: Hong Kong Cinema*, (London: Verso, 1999), p. 36. For more on Hong Kong "crisis cinema," see Tony Williams, "Space, Place, and Spectacle: The Crisis Cinema of John Woo," *Cinema Journal* 36:2 (Winter 1997), pp. 67–84. Information on film credits cited throughout this book has been taken from the Internet Movie Database, http://www.imdb.com/.

2. For more on John Woo's transnational productions, see Anne Ciecko, "Transnational Action: John Woo, Hong Kong, Hollywood," in Sheldon Hsiao-peng Lu, ed., *Transnational Chinese Cinemas: Identity, Nationhood, Gender* (Honolulu: University of Hawaii Press, 1997), pp. 221–238. Also, see Lisa Odham Stokes and Michael Hoover, *City on Fire: Hong Kong Cinema*, (London: Verso, 1999).

3. Charles Leary, "What Goes Around, Comes Around: *Infernal Affairs II* and *III* and *Running on Karma*," *Senses of Cinema* (January 2004), http://www.sensesofcinema.com/contents/04/30/infernal_affairs_ii.html/. See also his review of the first film in the trilogy: Charles Leary, "*Infernal Affairs:* High Concept in Hong Kong," *Senses of*

Cinema (April 2003), http://www.sensesofcinema.com/contents/03/26/infernal_affairs.html. In addition to Ann Hui, Joyce Chan (who later collaborated with Ann Hui) wrote *Family: A Metamorphosis*, a popular television series against corruption produced in the 1970s. For more on this series, see Evans Chan, "Postmodernism and Hong Kong Cinema" *Postmodern Culture* 10: 3 (May, 2000), http://www3.iath.virginia.edu /pmc/text-only/issue.500/10.3chan.txt/.

4.   In fact, Andrew Lau, Manfred Wong, and Wong Jing were partners in the Best of the Best production company.

5.   For an appraisal of Wong Jing, see Yingjin Zhang, *Chinese National Cinema* (NY: Routledge, 2004), p. 265.

6.   For more on the background of cast and crew, see Tony Rayns, "Deep Cover," *Sight and Sound* (January 2004), http://www.bfi.org.uk/sightandsound/2004_01/infernalaffairs.php/.

7.   Aihwa Ong, *Flexible Citizenship: The Cultural Logics of Transnationality* (Durham, NC: Duke University Press, 1999).

8.   For more on *Hero*, see Evans Chan, "Zhang Yimou's *Hero* — The Temptations of Fascism," *Film International* no. 8 (March 2004), http://www.filmint.nu/netonly/eng/heroevanschan.htm/. Chen Kaige also made a very different film about the Emperor Qin, *The Emperor and the Assassin* (1998). For an insightful reading of this film, see Yingjin Zhang, *Screening China: Critical Interventions, Cinematic Reconfigurations, and the Transnational Imaginary in Contemporary Chinese Cinema* (Ann Arbor: Center for Chinese Studies, University of Michigan, 2002), pp. 320–322.

Chapter 2   Forgotten Times: Music, Memory, Time, and Space

1.   For more on the depiction of economic relations within Hong Kong cinema, see Gina Marchetti, "Buying American, Consuming Hong Kong: Cultural Commerce, Fantasies of Identity, and the Cinema," in Poshek Fu and David Desser, eds., *The Cinema of Hong Kong: History, Arts, Identity* (New York: Cambridge University Press, 2000), pp. 289–313.

2.   Pierre Bourdieu, *Distinction: A Social Critique of the Judgement of Taste*, trans. Richard Nice (Cambridge: Harvard University Press, 1984).

3. For clarity, throughout the book, the first film in the trilogy is referred to as *Infernal Affairs I*.

4. David Chase quoted in Ellen Wulfhorst, "'Sopranos' final season focus: Money — Creator Chase leaves door open for more," *CNN*, May 24, 2005, http://www.cnn.com/2005/SHOWBIZ/TV/05/24/leisure. sopranos.reut/index.html/.

5. Stokes and Hoover, p. 302.

6. The title of the song is sometimes translated as "Those Were the Days."

7. See Appendix 2.

8. The use of the flashback technique references an entire sub-history of the cinema's relationship to memory and the human psyche, see Maureen Turim, *Flashbacks in Film: Memory and History* (NY: Routledge, 1989).

9. Iain Chambers, "Maps, Movies, Musics, and Memory," in David B. Clarke, ed., *The Cinematic City* (London: Routledge, 1997), pp. 232–233 (230–40).

10. Edward Yang is also known for his keen interest in music. See Emilie Yueh-Yu Yeh, "Elvis, Allow Me to Introduce Myself: American Music and Neocolonialism in Taiwan Cinema," *Modern Chinese Literature and Culture* 15:1 (Spring 2003), pp. 1–28.

11. Fredric Jameson, *The Geopolitical Aesthetic: Cinema and Space in the World System* (Bloomington: Indiana University Press, 1995).

12. For more on the centrality of Teresa Teng to *Comrades'* narrative, see Linda Chiu-han Lai, "Film and Enigmatization: Nostalgia, Nonsense, and Remembering," in Esther C. M. Yau, ed., *At Full Speed: Hong Kong Cinema in a Borderless World* (Minneapolis: University of Minnesota Press, 2001), pp. 231–250; Sheldon H. Lu, "Filming Diaspora and Identity: Hong Kong and 1997," in Poshek Fu and David Desser, eds., *The Cinema of Hong Kong: History, Arts, Identity* (NY: Cambridge University Press, 2000), pp. 273–288.

13. Leung also worked with Hou on *Flowers of Shanghai* (1998).

14. Shen Shiao-Ying, "Obtuse Music and Nebulous Males: The Haunting Presence of Taiwan in Hong Kong Films of the 1990s," in Laikwan Pang and Day Wong, eds., *Masculinities and Hong Kong Cinema* (Hong Kong: Hong Kong University Press, 2005), p. 135 (118–135). For a specific discussion of the "Taiwan Factor" in the Hong Kong

gangster genre, see Karen Fang, *John Woo's A Better Tomorrow* (Hong Kong: Hong Kong University Press, 2004).

15. For more on Chinese masculinity, see Kam Louie, *Theorizing Chinese Masculinity: Society and Gender in China* (Cambridge: Cambridge University Press, 2002).

16. For more on the uncanny in Hong Kong film, see Esther M. K. Cheung, "The City that Haunts: The Uncanny in Fruit Chan's *Made in Hong Kong*," in Esther M. K. Cheung and Chu Yiu-wai, eds., *Between Home and World: A Reader in Hong Kong Cinema* (Oxford: Oxford University Press, 2004), pp. 352–368. For more on the uncanny in relation to allegory in Hong Kong film, see Bliss Cua Lim, "Spectral Times: The Ghost Film as Historical Allegory," *positions: east asian cultures critique* 9:2 (Fall 2001), pp. 287–329.

17. With respect to this crisis in masculinity, *Infernal Affairs* seems to reference John Woo's oeuvre and then move off in a different direction. For more on men/masculinity in the films of John Woo, see Julian Stringer, "'Your Tender Smiles Give Me Strength': Paradigms of Masculinity in John Woo's *A Better Tomorrow* and *The Killer*," *Screen* 38:1 (Spring 1997), pp. 25–41.

18. The disabled hero has been an important trope in John Woo's cinema as well, see Anthony Enns, "The Spectacle of Disabled Masculinity in John Woo's 'Heroic Bloodshed' Films," *Quarterly Review of Film and Video* 17:2 (June 2000), pp. 137–145.

19. Ackbar Abbas has remarked on nostalgia in Hong Kong film in *Hong Kong: Culture and Politics of Disappearance* (Minneapolis: University of Minnesota Press, 1997). For more on Hong Kong's "nostalgia" cinema, see Rey Chow, "A Souvenir of Love," *Modern Chinese Literature* 7:2 (Fall 1993), pp. 59–78; Natalia Chan Sui Hung, "Rewriting History: Hong Kong Nostalgia Cinema and Its Social Practice," in Poshek Fu and David Desser, eds., *The Cinema of Hong Kong: History, Arts, Identity* (NY: Cambridge University Press, 2000), pp. 253–272; Linda Chiu-han Lai, "Film and Enigmatization: Nostalgia, Nonsense, and Remembering," in Esther C. M. Yau, ed., *At Full Speed: Hong Kong Cinema in a Borderless World* (Minneapolis: University of Minnesota Press, 2001), pp. 231–250. Although the "nostalgia films" discussed by these authors generally refer to films

set in the 1930s to 1960s, a case can be made for a new turn in nostalgia for the 1980s in Hong Kong film culture with films like *Infernal Affairs.*

20. Fredric Jameson, "Postmodernism and Consumer Culture," in Hal Foster, ed., *The Anti-Aesthetic: Essays on Postmodern Culture.* (Port Townsend, Washington: Bay Press, 1983), p. 116 (111–125). For more on the nostalgia film, see Vera Dika, *The Uses of Nostalgia: Recycled Culture in Contemporary Art and Film* (NY: Cambridge University Press, 2003).

21. They even call each other pet names — "Dumbo" and "Mickey Mouse" in one subtitled version of the film.

22. For a reading of *Face/Off* in relation to Hong Kong cinema and Chinese culture, see Kwai-Cheung Lo, *Chinese Face/Off: The Transnational Popular Culture of Hong Kong* (Urbana: University of Illinois Press, 2005). For a reading in relation to transnational cinema, see Chuck Kleinhans, "Terms of Transition: The Action Film, Postmodernism, and Issues of an East-West Perspective," in Jenny Kwok Wah Lau, ed., *Multiple Modernities: Cinemas and Popular Media in Transcultural East Asia* (Philadelphia: Temple University Press, 2003), pp. 167–178.

23. See Appendix 2.

24. See Karen Fang, *John Woo's A Better Tomorrow* (Hong Kong: Hong Kong University Press, 2004).

25. Jameson, "Postmodernism and Consumer Culture," pp. 115–116.

26. See Jillian Sandell, "Reinventing Masculinity: The Spectacle of Male Intimacy in the Films of John Woo," *Film Quarterly* 49:4 (Summer 1996), pp. 23–34.

27. For an eloquent discussion of the relationship between cinematic time, alienated labor, and modernity, see Mary Ann Doane, *The Emergence of Cinematic Time: Modernity, Contingency, the Archive* (Cambridge, MA: Harvard University Press, 2002).

28. Although translated this way in the subtitles, the phrase may be better represented by something more like: "He who lives by the sword, dies by the sword."

29. Mikhail Bakhtin, *The Dialogic Imagination*, trans. Caryl Emerson and Michael Holquist (Austin: University of Texas Press, 1981), p. 250.

30. Ibid, p. 85.
31. Martin Heidegger, *Being and Time*, trans. John Macquarrie and Edward Robinson (Oxford: Blackwell, 1962). Many scholars have investigated the relationship between Heidegger's philosophy and Nazi political convictions. For a discussion of how his thoughts on time relate specifically to his fascism, see David Harvey, *The Condition of Postmodernity: An Enquiry into the Origins of Cultural Change* (Oxford: Basil Blackwell, 1989).
32. For more on the usefulness of the chronotope to film analysis, see Michael V. Montgomery, *Carnivals and Commonplaces: Bakhtin's Chronotope, Cultural Studies, and Film* (NY: Peter Lang, 1994) and Robert Stam, *Subversive Pleasures: Bakhtin, Cultural Criticism, Film* (Baltimore: Johns Hopkins University Press, 1992).
33. Fredric Jameson, *The Geopolitical Aesthetic: Cinema and Space in the World System* (Bloomington: Indiana University Press, 1995), p. 3.
34. The chronotope associated with *Infernal Affairs III* bears a striking resemblance to the chronotope of life in exile explored in Hamid Naficy, *An Accented Cinema: Exilic and Diasporic Filmmaking* (Princeton: Princeton University Press, 2001), p. 191.
35. Robert Warshow, *The Immediate Experience* (Cambridge: Harvard University Press, 2001).
36. For information on cross-border criminal law, see H. L. Fu, "The Impact of the Chinese Criminal Law in Hong Kong," in Robert Ash, Peter Ferdinand, Brian Hook, and Robin Porter, eds., *Hong Kong in Transition: One Country, Two Systems* (London: Routledge Curzon, 2002), pp. 149–160.
37. In other postmodern films, time and memory complicate the action (e.g., *Blade Runner*, 1982, *Total Recall*, 1990).
38. Robert Warshow, *The Immediate Experience* (Cambridge: Harvard University Press, 2001), p. 101.
39. Yingchi Chu, *Hong Kong Cinema: Coloniser, Motherland, and Self* (London: Routledge Curzon, 2003), p. 130.
40. For a definition, see Saskia Sassen, *The Global City* (Princeton, NJ: Princeton University Press, 1991).
41. Marc Auge, *Non-Places: Introduction to an Anthropology of Supermodernity* (London: Verso, 1995), p. 79.

42. Building on Rem Koolhaas's notion of the Generic City, Ackbar Abbas sees Hong Kong in much the same way in Ackbar Abbas, "Cinema, the City, and the Cinematic," in Linda Krause and Patrice Petro, eds., *Global Cities: Cinema, Architecture, and Urbanism in the Digital Age* (New Brunswick, NJ: Rutgers University Press, 2003), pp. 142–156.

43. Yingjin Zhang, *Screening China: Critical Interventions, Cinematic Reconfigurations, and the Transnational Imaginary in Contemporary Chinese Cinema* (Ann Arbor: Center for Chinese Studies, University of Michigan, 2002), p. 308. Zhang draws here on the work of Lin Wenchi, "The Representation of Taipei in Taiwanese Films," in Ru-Shou Robert Chen and Gene-Fon Liao, eds., *Focus on Taipei through Cinema* (Taipei: Wanxiang, 1995), in Chinese, and Michel de Certeau, *The Practice of Everyday Life*, trans. Steven Rendall (Berkeley: University of California Press, 1984).

44. For a discussion of gender, the cinema, and the postmodern city, see Elisabeth Mahoney, "'The People in Parentheses': Space under Pressure in the Post-Modern City," in David B. Clarke, ed., *The Cinematic City* (London: Routledge, 1997), pp. 168–185.

45. Jane Jacobs, *The Death and Life of Great American Cities* (NY: Vintage, 1992, originally published in 1961).

46. Ackbar Abbas, *Hong Kong: Culture and the Politics of Disappearance*, p. 67.

47. Ibid, pp. 75–76.

48. David Harvey, *The Condition of Postmodernity: An Enquiry into the Origins of Cultural Change*, p. 5.

49. Mark Shiel, "Cinema and the City in History and Theory," in Mark Shiel and Tony Fitzmaurice, eds., *Cinema and the City: Film and Urban Societies in a Global Context* (Oxford: Blackwell, 2001), p. 12 (1–18).

Chapter 3   Allegories of Hell: Moral Tales and National Shadows

1. "Dharma Movie Review: *Infernal Affairs I* & *II:* The Path to Continuous Hell," http://www.moonpointer.com/movies/infernalaffairs.htm/.

2. See Martin Booth, *The Dragon Syndicates: The Global Phenomenon of the Triads* (NY: Carroll and Graf Publishers, Inc., 1999). See also Sterling Seagrave, *Lords of the Rim* (London: Corgi, Bantam, 1995).

3. For a discussion of Confucius and Guan Gong as models of Chinese masculinity, see Kam Louie, *Theorising Chinese Masculinity: Society and Gender in China* (Cambridge: Cambridge University Press, 2002).

4. A very different reading of this conflict between the rule of law and the rule of blood will be discussed below.

5. Fredric Jameson, "Third World Literature in the Era of Multinational Capitalism," *Social Text* 15 (1986), pp. 65–88; Aijaz Ahmad, "Jameson's Rhetoric of Otherness and the 'National Allegory'," *Social Text* 17 (1987), pp. 3–25; Ian Buchanan, "National Allegory Today: A Return to Jameson," *New Formations* 51:1 (December 2003), pp. 66–79. For an example of the use of Jameson on national allegory to analyze Chinese film, see Yingjin Zhang, *Screening China*, op. cit.

6. Sheldon H. Lu, "Filming Diaspora and Identity: Hong Kong and 1997," Poshek Fu and David Desser, eds., *The Cinema of Hong Kong: History, Arts, Identity* (NY: Cambridge University Press, 2000), pp. 273–288.

7. Stephen Teo, *Hong Kong Cinema: The Extra Dimensions* (London: BFI, 1997), p. 207. Esther Yau, "Border Crossing: Mainland China's Presence in Hong Kong Cinema," in Nick Browne, Paul G. Pickowicz, Vivian Sobchack, and Esther Yau, eds., *New Chinese Cinemas: Forms, Identities, Politics* (NY: Cambridge University Press, 1994), p. 181 (pp. 180–201).

8. Benedict Anderson, *Imagined Communities: Reflections on the Origin and Spread of Nationalism* (London: Verso, 1991).

9. The much ballyhooed truism that Hong Kong is the "freest" economy on earth hides a history of complex relations between colonial government, global capitalism, and Hong Kong's place within the world economy. For a case study on government intervention in the wake of the 1997 financial crisis, see Charles Goodhart and Lu Dai, *Intervention to Save Hong Kong: The Authorities' Counter-Speculation in Financial Markets* (Oxford: Oxford University Press, 2003). For further analysis of the economic crisis, see Y. C. Jao, *The Asian Financial Crisis and the Ordeal of Hong Kong* (Westport, CT: Quorum Books, 2001).

10. For more on this point, see Yingchi Chu, *Hong Kong Cinema: Coloniser, Motherland, and Self* (London: Routledge Curzon, 2003). In this book, Chu examines the Jackie Chan vehicles *Project A* and *Project A (Part II)* as fantasies involving Hong Kong as a mediator between British and Chinese interests through the operation of the colonial police/coast guard. The book also explores the complex relationship between Hong Kong triads, Mainland gangs, and the Hong Kong police in *The Long Arm of the Law*.

11. For a definition of Greater China, see William A. Callahan, *Contingent States: Greater China and Transnational Relations* (Minneapolis: University of Minnesota Press, 2004). Chapter 5 deals specifically with Hong Kong.

12. For more on Hong Kong's political economy, see William Overholt, "Hong Kong at the Crossroads," Testimony Presented to the House Committee on International Relations, Subcommittee on Asia and the Pacific, June 23, 2004, Rand Corporation, http://www.rand.org/pubs/testimonies/2005/RAND_CT228.pdf/.

13. Roland Barthes, "Myth Today," *Mythologies*, trans. Annette Lavers (NY: Hill and Wang, 1972), p. 116 (109–159).

14. Kabir Chhibber, "Timeline: Hong Kong," *Guardian*, July 1, 2002, http://www.guardian.co.uk/china/story/0,7369,747459,00.html; See also, Hong Kong Timeline, http://timelines.ws/countries/HONG_KONG.HTML/.

15. For a collection of perspectives on the political and economic consequences of the handover, see James C. Hsiung, ed., *Hong Kong and the Super Paradox: Life after Return to China* (NY: St. Martin's Press, 2000).

16. Jerome Silbergeld, *China into Film: Frames of Reference in Contemporary Chinese Cinema* (London: Reaktion Books, 1999).

17. For a definition of the "post-national," see Arjun Appadurai, *Modernity at Large: Cultural Dimensions of Globalization* (Minneapolis: University of Minnesota Press, 1996).

18. Entry in *Nationmaster*, http://www.nationmaster.com/encyclopedia/Chris-Patten/. Attributed to Lu Ping (1995) and quoted in *HK Magazine*, June 16, 2006, p. 54.

19. Hawaii, long before US statehood, had a history of Chinese triad

activity, including Sun Yat-sen's contact with the Hawaiian triads during his time as an insurgent against the Qing Dynasty. See Martin Booth, *The Dragon Syndicates: The Global Phenomenon of the Triads* (NY: Carroll and Graf Publishers, Inc., 1999). For more on the triads in North America, see Peter Huston, *Tongs, Gangs, and Triads: Chinese Crime Groups in North America* (Boulder, CO: Paladin Press, 2001).

20. See Benjamin T. M. Liu, *The Hong Kong Triad Societies: Before and After the 1997 Change-over* (Hong Kong: Net e-Publishing, Ltd., 2001), p. 215.

21. See Mayfair Yang, *Gifts, Favors, and Banquets: The Art of Social Relationships in China* (Ithaca, NY: Cornell University Press, 1994); Gina Marchetti, "Taiwanese Triads in the Transnational Imagination: *Mahjong* and *Goodbye South, Goodbye*," *Film International*, No. 9 (2004), pp. 28–41.

22. See Peter Wesley-Smith, "Judicial Autonomy under Hong Kong's Basic Law," in Robert Ash, Peter Ferdinand, Brian Hook, and Robin Porter, eds., *Hong Kong in Transition: One Country, Two Systems* (London: Routledge Curzon, 2002), pp. 161–174.

23. Quoted anonymously in Bob Beatty, *Democracy, Asian Values, and Hong Kong: Evaluating Political Elite Beliefs* (Westport, CT: Praeger, 2003), p. 97.

24. Kevin Sinclair and Nelson Ng Kwok-cheung, *Asia's Finest Marches On: Policing Hong Kong from 1841 into the 21st Century* (Hong Kong: Kevin Sinclair Associates Limited, 1997). See also H. J. Lethbridge, *Hard Graft in Hong Kong: Scandal, Corruption, and the ICAC* (Hong Kong: Oxford University Press, 1985).

25. William H. Overholt, p. 16, http://www.rand.org/pubs/testimonies/2005/RAND_CT228.pdf/. For more information on economic changes in the HKSAR, e.g., CEPA (Closer Economic Partnership Agreement), see http://cepa.tdctrade.com/.

26. For an analysis of the actual economy of triad businesses, see Yiu Kong Chu, *The Triads as Business* (London: Routledge, 2000).

27. For more on 14K, see Benjamin T. M. Liu, *The Hong Kong Triad Societies: Before and After the 1997 Change-over* (Hong Kong: Net e-Publishing, Ltd., 2001).

28. Kevin Sinclair and Nelson Ng Kwok-cheung, op. cit.

29. Fenton Bresler, *The Chinese Mafia* (Middlesex: Hamlyn Paperbacks, 1981).

30. Jean-Francois Lyotard, *The Postmodern Condition: A Report on Knowledge* (Minneapolis: University of Minnesota Press, 1984).

Chapter 4   Postmodern Allegory: The Global Economy and New Technologies

1. Fredric Jameson, *Postmodernism: Or, the Cultural Logic of Late Capitalism* (Durham: Duke University Press, 1991), p. 168. For a perceptive reading of Hong Kong *wu xia pian* as postmodern allegories, see Bhaskar Sarkar, "Hong Kong Hysteria: Martial Arts Tales from a Mutating World," in Esther C. M. Yau, ed., *At Full Speed: Hong Kong Cinema in a Borderless World* (Minneapolis: University of Minnesota Press, 2001), pp. 159–176.

2. See Esther M. K. Cheung and Chu Yiu-wai, eds., "Introduction: Between Home and World," in *Between Home and World: A Reader in Hong Kong Cinema* (Oxford: Oxford University Press), pp. xi–xxxv.

3. Esther C. M. Yau, "Introduction: Hong Kong Cinema in a Borderless World," in Esther C. M. Yau, ed., *At Full Speed: Hong Kong Cinema in a Borderless World* (Minneapolis: University of Minnesota Press, 2001), p. 4 (1–28).

4. James A. Steintrager, "An Unworthy Subject: Slaughter, Cannibalism and Postcoloniality," in Laikwan Pang and Day Wong, eds., *Masculinities and Hong Kong Cinema* (Hong Kong: Hong Kong University Press, 2005), p. 155 (155–174).

5. Jameson, *Geopolitical Aesthetic*, p. 5.

6. Karl Marx, *Capital: A Critique of Political Economy, Vol. I: The Process of Capitalist Production*, trans. Samuel Moore and Edward Aveling, ed. Frederick Engels (NY: International, 1967), p. 72. For more on the commodity in recent Hong Kong cinema, see Gina Marchetti, "Buying American, Consuming Hong Kong: Cultural Commerce, Fantasies of Identity, and the Cinema," in Poshek Fu and David Desser,

eds., *The Cinema of Hong Kong: History, Arts, Identity* (New York: Cambridge University Press, 2000), pp. 289–313.

7. George Myserson, *Heidegger, Habermas, and the Mobile Phone* (Cambridge: Icon Books, 2001).

8. Jacques Derrida, *Archive Fever: A Freudian Impression*, trans. Eric Prenowitz (Chicago: University of Chicago Press, 1998), pp. 19–20. With the turn of the century, there has been a resurgence of interest in memory, amnesia, and technology; for more on these themes, see Andreas Huyssen, *Present Pasts: Urban Palimpsests and the Politics of Memory* (Stanford, CA: Stanford University Press, 2003).

9. Derrida, p. 90.

Chapter 5   Identity as Static: Surveillance, Psychoanalysis, and Performance

1. Deleuze, *Cinema 1*, p. 210.

2. Jean Baudrillard, "The Ecstasy of Communication," translated by John Johnston, in Hal Foster, ed., *The Anti-Aesthetic: Essays on Postmodern Culture* (Post Townsend, WA: Bay Press, 1983), p. 127 (126–134). David Cronenberg's *Videodrome* (1983) comes to mind as well.

3. Teo, *Hong Kong Cinema: The Extra Dimension*, p. 250.

4. "Encyclopedia: Hong Kong Police Force," Nationmaster.com, http://www.nationmaster.com/encyclopedia/Hong-Kong-Police/.

5. Baudrillard, "Ecstasy of Communication", p. 133.

6. Jameson, "Postmodernism and Consumer Culture," p. 120. Jameson also points out that it really does not matter if the Enlightenment subject ever actually existed or was always a fiction. It only matters that it only operates as a fiction within postmodern culture.

7. Jameson, "Postmodernism and Consumer Culture," p. 125.

8. Yingchi Chu, *Hong Kong Cinema: Coloniser, Motherland, and Self* (London: Routledge Curzon, 2003), p. 129.

9. Zhang, *Chinese National Cinema*, p. 269.

10. Laikwan Pang, "Post-1997 Hong Kong Masculinity," in Laikwan Pang and Day Wong, eds., *Masculinities and Hong Kong Cinema* (Hong Kong: Hong Kong University Press, 2005), p. 36 (35–55).

11. In many ways, Chan resembles the troubled, Romantic hero described in Chuck Kleinhans, "Terms of Transition: The Action Film, Postmodernism, and Issues of an East-West Perspective," op. cit.

12. Fredric Jameson, *Postmodernism: Or, the Cultural Logic of Late Capitalism* (NY: Verso, 1991), p. 156, p. 364.

13. Gilles Deleuze and Felix Guatarri, *Anti-Oedipus: Capitalism and Schizophrenia*, trans. Robert Hurley, Mark Seem, and Helen R. Lane (Minneapolis: University of Minnesota Press, 1983), p. 2. There is considerable scholarly discussion on various uses of "schizophrenia" to describe the postmodern condition, including Fredric Jameson, *Postmodernism: Or, the Cultural Logic of Late Capitalism*. For a comparison of Deleuze and Guattari and Jameson on the topic, see Jonah Peretti, "Capitalism and Schizophrenia: Contemporary Visual Culture and the Acceleration of Identity Formation/Dissolution," *Negations* (Winter 1996), http://www.datawranglers.com/negations/issues/96w/96w_peretti.html/.

14. Baudrillard, p. 127.

15. See Stuart Hall, "New Ethnicities," in David Morley and Kuan-Hsing Chen, eds. *Stuart Hall: Critical Dialogues in Cultural Studies* (NY: Routledge, 1996), pp. 441–449.

16. See Joan Riviere, "Womanliness as Masquerade," in Victor Burgin, James Donald and Cora Kaplan, eds., *Formations of Fantasy* (London and New York: Methuen, 1986, originally published in 1929), pp. 35–44; Mary Ann Doane. "Film and the Masquerade: Theorising the Female Spectator," *Screen*, 23: 3–4 (September/October 1982), pp. 74–87.

17. W. E. B. Du Bois, *The Souls of Black Folk*, ed. Henry Louis Gates, Jr. and Terri Hume Oliver (NY: Norton, 1999); Frantz Fanon, *Black Skin, White Masks*, trans. Charles Lam Markmann (NY: Grove Press, 1967).

18. See Judith Butler, *Gender Trouble: Feminism and the Subversion of Identity* (NY: Routledge, 1990).

19. Homi Bhabha, *The Location of Culture* (London: Routledge, 1994).

20. For a discussion of identity in post-1997 Hong Kong cinema, see Chu Yiu Wai, "Hybridity and (G)local Identity in Postcolonial Hong Kong Cinema," in Sheldon H. Lu and Emilie Yueh-Yu Yeh, eds., *Chinese-Language Film: Historiography, Poetics, Politics* (Honolulu: University of Hawaii Press, 2005), pp. 312–328.

21. John Berger, *Ways of Seeing* (London: BBC and Penguin, 1972). Also note Bertolucci's *The Last Emperor* (1987) and the occupation of a "feminized space" by the Chinese male in Rey Chow, *Woman and Chinese Modernity: The Politics of Reading Between West and East* (Minneapolis: University of Minnesota Press, 1991).

22. Andreas Huyssen, *After the Great Divide: Modernism, Mass Culture, Postmodernism* (Indiana University Press, 1986).

23. Bryan Chang, "Never Running Out of Choices (in A World Without Method)," trans. Sam Ho, *Andy Lau: Actor in Focus* (Hong Kong: Hong Kong International Film Festival Society, 2005), p. 67 (62–67).

24. Michel Foucault, *Discipline and Punish: The Birth of the Prison*, trans. Alan Sheridan (London: Allen Lane, Penguin Books, 1977).

25. Mark Poster, *The Mode of Information: Poststructuralism and Social Context* (Chicago: University of Chicago Press, 1990), p. 93. The same point is made in Kevin Robins and Frank Webster, *Times of Technoculture: From the Information Society to the Virtual Life* (London: Routledge, 1999).

26. For a discussion of consumerism and television as part of the postmodern condition, see Margaret Morse, "An Ontology of Everyday Distraction: The Freeway, the Mall, and Television," in Patricia Mellencamp, ed., *Logics of Television: Essays in Cultural Criticism* (Bloomington: Indiana University Press, 1990), pp. 193–221.

27. Slavoj Zizek, *Enjoy Your Symptom! Jacques Lacan in Hollywood and Out* (NY: Routledge, 1992), p. 34 and p. 53.

28. Dorinne Kondo, *About Face: Performing Race in Fashion and Theater* (NY: Routledge, 1997), p. 7.

29. Gilles Deleuze, *Cinema 2: The Time-Image*, trans. Hugh Tomlinson (Minneapolis: University of Minnesota Press, 1989), pp. 19–20.

30. Lee Cheuk-To, "Introduction," *Andy Lau: Actor in Focus* (Hong Kong: Hong Kong International Film Festival Society, 2005), p. 3.

31. Thomas Shin, Athena Sui, Bryan Chang, "Interviewing Andy Lau," *Andy Lau: Actor in Focus* (Hong Kong: Hong Kong International Film Festival Society, 2005), p. 44 (40–55).

32. For more on Leung's character, see Wimal Dissanayake, *Wong Kar-wai's Ashes of Time* (Hong Kong: Hong Kong University Press, 2003).

33. For more on the Leung character, see Jeremy Tambling, *Wong Kar-wai's Happy Together* (Hong Kong: Hong Kong University Press, 2003).

34. Ryan Gilbey, "The Leung View," *The Sunday Times* (UK), 29 February 2004, http://www.tonyleung.org/news/interview2004_1.shtml/.

35. Fredric Dannen and Barry Long, *Hong Kong Babylon: An Insider's Guide to the Hollywood of the East* (London: Faber and Faber, 1997), pp. 138–141.

36. For a detailed reading of *The Untold Story*, see James A. Steintrager, "An Unworthy Subject: Slaughter, Cannibalism and Postcoloniality," in Laikwan Pang and Day Wong, eds., *Masculinities and Hong Kong Cinema* (Hong Kong: Hong Kong University Press, 2005), pp. 155–174.

Chapter 6   Thieves and Pirates: Beyond "Auteur" Cinema

1. Gilles Deleuze, *Cinema 1: The Movement Image*, trans. Hugh Tomlinson and Barbara Habberjam (Minneapolis: University of Minnesota Press, 1986), pp. 208–209.

2. Stephen Teo, *Hong Kong Cinema: The Extra Dimensions* (London: BFI, 1997), p. 233.

3. Ackbar Abbas, *Hong Kong: Culture and the Politics of Disappearance*, p. 36.

4. For a definition of the "televisual" ("videographic" as opposed to the "cinematic"), see John Thornton Caldwell, *Televisuality: Style, Crisis, and Authority in American Television* (New Brunswick, NJ: Rutgers University Press, 1995).

5. It plays with the shift from Debord's "society of the spectacle" or Foucault's "panoptican" to Baudrillard's "hyperreal" realm of "simulation." See Jean Baudrillard, "The Procession of Simulacra," in *Simulacra and Simulation*, trans. Sheila Faria Glaser (Ann Arbor: University of Michigan Press, 1994, 1981), pp. 1–42.

6. For a history of Hong Kong's transnational film connections, see Law Kar and Frank Bren (with Sam Ho), *Hong Kong Cinema: A Cross-Cultural View* (Lanham, MD: Scarecrow Press, 2004).

7. See Liang Hai-Chiang, "Hong Kong Cinema's 'Taiwan Factor'," Law Kar, ed., *Fifty Years of Electric Shadows, 21st Hong Kong International Film Festival*, trans. Yatsen Chan (Hong Kong: Urban Council, 1997), pp. 158–163. See also, Kwai-cheung Lo, *Chinese Face/Off: The Transnational Popular Culture of Hong Kong* (Urbana: University of Illinois Press, 2005), pp. 106–107.

8. For a discussion of this aspect of film history, see Adam Knee, "Thailand in the Hong Kong Cinematic Imagination," *Hong Kong/Hollywood at the Borders: Alternative Perspectives, Alternative Cinemas*, University of Hong Kong, April 2004, unpublished paper.

9. Warner Brothers, of course, has a long history of involvement with Hong Kong including co-productions beginning in the 1970s with Golden Harvest.

10. That Coppola should explore similar themes in *The Godfather* and *The Conversation* regarding a crisis in American society comes as no surprise, and neither does the fact that *Infernal Affairs* seems to reference both films for a similar reason.

11. Alison Veneto, "The Modern Hong Kong Triad Film: Part II," *Movie Poop Shoot*, May 26, 2006, http://www.moviepoopshoot.com/intrigue/26.html/.

12. See Appendix 2.

13. For more on the series, see David Bordwell, *Planet Hong Kong: Popular Cinema and the Art of Entertainment* (Cambridge, MA: Harvard University Press, 2000).

14. Although not mentioned by name, it is clearly the series lawmaker Benjamin T. M. Liu refers to when he complains about films that fueled the triad push to recruit members from Hong Kong public schools. See Benjamin T. M. Liu, *The Hong Kong Triad Societies: Before and After the 1997 Change-over* (Hong Kong: Net e-Publishing, Ltd., 2001).

15. For a chronology of these events, see Benjamin T. M. Liu, op. cit.

16. Fredric Dannen and Barry Long, *Hong Kong Babylon: An Insider's Guide to the Hollywood of the East* (London: Faber and Faber, 1997), p. 44. See also Lisa Odham Stokes and Michael Hoover, *City on Fire: Hong Kong Cinema*, (London: Verso, 1999). Of course, gangsters have long been a part of other lucrative film industries, including

Hollywood, see Peter Bondanella, *Hollywood Italians: Dagos, Palookas, Romeos, Wise Guys, and Sopranos* (NY: Continuum, 2004). Hong Kong filmmakers have also dealt directly on screen with the impact of triads in the film industry (e.g., *Stuntwoman/Ah Kam*, 1996; *Viva Erotica*, 1996).

17. *Young and Dangerous IV* (1997) specifically locates part of its action in Tuen Mun and includes a detailed history of Tuen Mun by one of the film's protagonists. Quoted in Stokes and Hoover, pp. 83–84.

18. This anti-individualism may, indeed, put *Infernal Affairs'* creators in a better position to market themselves globally as "design professionals." See Steve Fore, "Home, Migration, Identity: Hong Kong Filmmakers Join the Chinese Diaspora," in Law Kar, ed., *Fifty Years of Electric Shadows: Report of Conference on Hong Kong Cinema*. (Hong Kong: The 21st Hong Kong International Film Festival, Urban Council of Hong Kong, 1997), pp. 130–135.

19. For discussions of the salient characteristics of Wong Kar-wai's oeuvre, see Ackbar Abbas, "The Erotics of Disappointment," in Jean-Marc Lalanne, David Martinez, Ackbar Abbas, and Jimmy Ngai, *Wong Kar-wai* (Paris: Dis Voir, 1997), pp. 39–81; Robert M. Payne, "Ways of Seeing Wild: The Cinema of Wong Kar-wai," *Jump Cut* No. 44 (Fall 2001), http://www.ejumpcut.org/archive/jc44.2001/payne%20for%20site/wongkarwai1.html/; Curtis K. Tsui, "Subjective Culture and History: The Ethnographic Cinema of Wong Kar-wai," *Asian Cinema* 7:2 (Winter 1995), pp. 93–124; Stephen Teo, *Wong Kar-wai* (London: BFI, 2005); Peter Brunette, *Wong Kar-wai* (Urbana: University of Illinois Press, 2005).

20. For more on video piracy in Hong Kong, see Shujen Wang, *Framing Piracy: Globalization and Film Distribution in Greater China* (Lanham, MD: Rowman and Littlefield Publishers, Inc., 2003).

21. See Laikwan Pang, "Piracy/Privacy: The Despair of Cinema and Collectivity in China," *boundary 2* 31:3 (Fall 2004), pp. 101–124.

22. Walter Benjamin, *One-Way Street*, trans. Edmund Jephcott and Kingsley Shorter (London: Verso, 1979, 1997), p. 50.

23. Borys Kit, "Gere Tends 'Flock' for Hong Kong Helmer," *Reuters/Hollywood Reporter*, August 3, 2005, http://news.yahoo.com/s/nm/20050803/film_nm/gere_dc/.

24. Evans Chan, "Postmodernism and Hong Kong Cinema," *Postmodern Culture* 10: 3 (May, 2000), http://www3.iath.virginia.edu/pmc/text-only/issue.500/10.3chan.txt/.

Credits

Infernal Affairs/Wu Jian Dao/Mou Gaan Dou (無間道)

Hong Kong 2002

Directors
Andrew Lau (Lau Wai-keung)
Alan Mak (Mak Siu-fai)

Scriptwriters
Alan Mak (Mak Siu-Fai)
Felix Chong

Line Producers
Ellen Chang
Lorraine Ho

Credits complied from the Internet Movie Database, www.imdb.com, and from the DVD versions of the films from Media Asia.

Producer
Lau Wai-keung

Assistant Production Managers
Bonnie Shum
Wendy Chan

Executive Producers
Nansun Shi
John Chong

Original Music
Chan Kwong-wing

Cinematographers
Christopher Doyle
Lai Yiu-fai
Lau Wai-keung (as Andrew Lau)

Film Editors
Pang Ching-hei
Danny Pang

Production Designer
Choo Sung-pong

Art Directors
Wong Ching-ching
Choo Sung-pong

Costume Designer
Lee Pik-kwan

Production Manager
Ronald Wong

First Assistant Director
Chan Wai-hung

Sound
Kinson Tsang

Dolby Film Sound Consultant
Mark Kenna

Visual Effects Supervisors
Eddy Wong
Victor Wong

Visual Consultant
Christopher Doyle

Action Choreographer
Dion Lam

Steadicam Operator
Raymond Lam

Gaffer
Wong Chi-ming

Production Companies
Basic Pictures
Media Asia Films Ltd.

Cast

Andy Lau (劉德華)	as Lau Kin-ming (劉建明)
Tony Leung Chiu-wai (梁朝偉)	as Chan Wing-yan (陳永仁)
Anthony Wong Chau-sang (黃秋生)	as SP Wong (黃志誠)
Eric Tsang (曾志偉)	as Sam (韓琛)
Kelly Chen (陳慧琳)	as Dr. Lee Sum Yee (李心兒)
Sammi Cheng (鄭秀文)	as Mary, Lau's wife (韓琛之妻)
Edison Chen (陳冠希)	as Young Lau Kin-ming (少年劉建明)
Shawn Yue (余文樂)	as Young Chan Wing-yan (少年陳永仁)

Elva Hsiao (蕭亞軒)	as May
Chapman To (杜汶澤)	as Keung (傻強)
Lam Ka-tung (林家棟)	as Inspector Billy (大B/林國平)
Ng Ting-yip (吳庭燁)	as Inspector Cheung (張督察)
Wan Chi-keung (尹志強)	as SP Leung (梁警司)
Dion Lam (林迪安)	as Del Piero (迪比亞路)
Hui Kam-fung (許金鋒)	as cadet school principal (警校校長)
Courtney Wu (利沙華)	as stereo shop owner (音響舖老闆)
Lee Wah-chu (李華柱)	as chief inspector (總警司)
Au Hin-wai (區軒偉)	as Elephant (大象)
Li Tin-cheung (李天翔)	as Double 8 (孖八)
Chaucharew Wichai	as Thai drug dealer (泰國毒品賣家)
Cheung Yuk-sun (張旭燊)	as cadet school instructor (警校教官)
Hui On-tat (許安達)	as SP Chan (陳警司)
Ho Wing-ling (何永寧)	as superintendent (警司)
Chung Wai-ho (何仲偉)	as Sam's follower (韓琛手下)
Wong Kam-hung (王錦洪)	as Sam's follower (韓琛手下)
Leung Ho-kei (梁浩楷)	as Sam's follower (韓琛手下)
Lee Yip-kin (李業健)	as Sam's follower (韓琛手下)
Lee Tze-ming (李子明)	as Sam's follower (韓琛手下)
So Wai-nam (蘇偉南)	as Sam's follower (韓琛手下)
Lai Chi-wai (黎志偉)	as Sam's follower (韓琛手下)
Wong Chi-wang (黃志宏)	as CIB Team (重案組警員)
Cheng Wing-yee (鄭穎儀)	as CIB Team (重案組警員)
Kui Mei-yee (瞿美儀)	as CIB Team (重案組警員)
Lam Po-loy (林溥來)	as CIB Team (重案組警員)
Mak Wai-kwok (麥偉幗)	as CIB Team (重案組警員)
Wong Yin-keung (黃燕強)	as CIB Team (重案組警員)
Yiu Man-kee (姚文基)	as CIB Team (重案組警員)
Yuen Wai-ho (袁偉豪)	as CIB Team (重案組警員)
Tony Ho (何華超)	as suspect (嫌疑犯)
Leung Chiu-yi (梁超怡)	as May's daughter (May的女兒)

Runtime

101 min / Hong Kong: 97 min (director's cut)

Infernal Affairs II/Wu Jian Dao II/Mou Gaan Dou II (無間道II)

Hong Kong 2003

Directors
Andrew Lau (Lau Wai-keung)
Alan Mak (Mak Siu-fai)

Scriptwriters
Alan Mak (Mak Siu-fai)
Felix Chong

Original Music
Chan Kwong-wing

Cinematographers
Lau Wai-keung (HKSC)
Ng Man-ching (HKSC)

Film Editors
Pang Ching-hei
Danny Pang

Sound Designer
Kinson Tsang

Sound Re-recording Mixer
Kinson Tsang

Visual Effects Supervisors
Eddy Wong
Victor Wong

Additional Music
Johannes Brahms (composer)

Steadicam Operator
Raymond Lam

Production Companies
Basic Pictures
Eastern Dragon Film Co. Ltd.
Media Asia Films Ltd.
Mediacorp Raintree Pictures

Cast

Edison Chen (陳冠希)	as Lau Kin-ming (劉建明)
Shawn Yue (余文樂)	as Chan Wing-yan (陳永仁)
Anthony Wong Chau-sang (黃秋生)	as SP Wong (黃志誠)
Francis Ng (吳鎮宇)	as Ngai Wing-hau (倪永孝)
Eric Tsang (曾志偉)	as Sam (韓琛)
Carina Lau (劉嘉玲)	as Mary, Sam's wife
Chapman To (杜汶澤)	as Keung (傻強)
Lin Hoi/Andrew Lin (連凱)	as Ngai's brother/Chung (倪永忠)
Roy Cheung (張耀揚)	as Law (羅雞)
Bey Logan	as Inspector Calvin
Ricardo Mamood	as parking lot dealer
Brandon Rhea	as private investigator
Teddy Chan (陳德森)	as Ching (文拯)
"Joe" Cheung Tung-cho (張同祖)	as Kwan (倪坤)
Fong Ping (方平)	as Gandhi (甘地)
Peter Ngor (敖志君)	as Negro (黑鬼)
Wai Ying-hung (惠英紅)	as Hau's sister (二家姐)
Chiu Chung-yue (趙頌茹)	as young Mary, Lau's wife
Hui Kam-fung (許金鋒)	as cadet school principal (警校校長)
Hu Jun (胡軍)	as SP Luk (陸啟昌)
Liu Kai-chi (廖啟智)	as Uncle John (三叔)
Wan Chi-keung (尹志強)	as SP Leung (梁警司)
Arthur Wong/Wong Ngok-tai (黃岳泰)	as Wah (國華)

Runtime
119 min

Infernal Affairs III/Wu Jian Dao III/Mou Gaan Dou III: Jung Gik Mou Gaan (無間道III: 終極無間)

Hong Kong 2003

Directors
Andrew Lau (Lau Wai-Keung)
Alan Mak (Mak Siu-Fai)

Scriptwriters
Alan Mak (Mak Siu-Fai)
Felix Chong

Original Music
Chan Kwong-wing

Cinematographers
Lau Wai-keung
Ng Man-Ching

Film Editors
Pang Ching-hei
Danny Pang

Camera Operator
Jimmy Wong

Steadicam Operator
Jimmy Wong

Production Companies
Basic Pictures
Eastern Dragon Film Co. Ltd.
Media Asia Films Ltd.

Cast

Andy Lau (劉德華)	as Lau Kin-ming (劉建明)
Tony Leung Chiu-wai (梁朝偉)	as Chan Wing-yan (陳永仁)
Leon Lai (黎明)	as SP Yeung (楊錦榮)
Kelly Chen (陳慧琳)	as Dr. Lee Sum Yee (李心兒)
Chen Daoming (陳道明)	as Shen (沈澄)
Anthony Wong Chau-sang (黃秋生)	as SP Wong (黃志誠)
Eric Tsang (曾志偉)	as Sam (韓琛)
Chapman To (杜汶澤)	as Keung (傻強)
Ng Ting-yip (吳庭燁)	as Inspector Cheung (張督察)
Wan Chi-keung (尹志強)	as SP Leung (梁警司)
Edison Chen (陳冠希)	as young Lau Kin-ming (少年劉建明)
Shawn Yue (余文樂)	as young Chan Wing-yan (少年陳永仁)
Sammi Cheng (鄭秀文)	as Mary #1, Lau's wife
Carina Lau (劉嘉玲)	as Mary #2, Sam's wife
Ka Tung Lam (林家棟)	as Inspector Billy (林國平)
Waise Lee (李子雄)	as Chun (陳俊)
Wan Yeung-ming (尹揚明)	as night club manager (夜總會經理)
Eddie Li (李雨陽)	as young Yeung (少年楊錦榮)
Courtney Wu (利沙華)	as stereo shop owner (音響舖老闆)
Dickson Yip Wai-chuen (葉偉全)	as security wing officer (保安科探員)
Lau Hing-keung (劉興權)	as security wing officer (保安科探員)
Zac Koo (高皓正)	as security wing officer (保安科探員)
Pan Wai-ming (彭偉明)	as security wing officer (保安科探員)
Louisa Ng (吳慧冰)	as security wing officer (保安科探員)
Sit Kam-wai (薛劍偉)	as security wing officer (保安科探員)
Huang Zhi-zhong (黃志忠)	as Liang (沈亮)

Runtime

118 min